# CRITICAL
# TECHNOLOGY
## ISSUES
### for
## SCHOOL
## LEADERS

## SUSAN BROOKS-YOUNG

**CORWIN PRESS**
A SAGE Publications Company
Thousand Oaks, California

*For information:*

Corwin Press
A Sage Publications Company
2455 Teller Road
Thousand Oaks, California 91320
www.corwinpress.com

Sage Publications Ltd.
1 Oliver's Yard
55 City Road
London EC1Y 1SP
United Kingdom

Sage Publications India Pvt. Ltd.
B-42, Panchsheel Enclave
Post Box 4109
New Delhi 110 017  India

Printed in the United States of America.

*Library of Congress Cataloging-in-Publication Data*

Brooks-Young, Susan.
Critical technology issues for school leaders/Susan Brooks-Young.
    p. cm.
Includes index.
ISBN 1-4129-2729-3 (cloth) — ISBN 1-4129-2730-7 (pbk.)
    1.  Educational technology. 2.  School administrators.  I.  Title.
LB1028.3.B764 2007
371.33—dc22

                                            2006001791


This book is printed on acid-free paper.

06   07   08   09   10   9   8   7   6   5   4   3   2   1

| | |
|---|---|
| *Acquisitions Editor:* | Elizabeth Brenkus |
| *Editorial Assistant:* | Desirée Enayati |
| *Production Editor:* | Jenn Reese |
| *Copy Editor:* | Cate Huisman |
| *Typesetter:* | C&M Digitals (P) Ltd. |
| *Proofreader:* | Joyce Li |
| *Indexer:* | Karen McKenzie |
| *Cover Designer:* | Michael Dubowe |

# *Contents*

# Acknowledgments

My first article appeared in a Peter Li Education Group publication in 1986. This was the beginning of a working relationship that's still going strong nearly 20 years later. During that time, I've worked with wonderful people on the staffs of several Peter Li publications. To attempt to list them all would guarantee that I would leave someone out, so I won't go there. However, I feel safe in expressing special gratitude to the editors of *Today's Catholic Teacher* and *Today's School*, the magazines in which the chapters in this book originally appeared as columns. So, thanks to Mary Noschang and Shannon O'Connor for giving me the opportunity to do the work I love, and for being great editors and good friends.

Coordinators and technicians from around the United States and two foreign countries responded to my request for the best troubleshooting tips for teachers and students to include in Chapter 18. Thanks to Paul R. Wood, Bishop Dunne Catholic School (Texas); Michael Dixon, Greene County Middle School (North Carolina); Ray Jones, Franklin Community Schools (Indiana); Demetri Orlando, Norwood School (Maryland); Mano Talaiver, Science Museum of Virginia (Virginia); Marilyn Mossman, Hillel Day School (Michigan); Laurie Jean Orszulak, Covenant Academy (New York); Kevin Oda, West Contra Costa Unified School District (California); Jennifer Wagner, Crossroads Christian School (California); Hilary Naylor, Oakland Unified School District (California); Helen Rape, Oakboro and Locust Elementary Schools (North Carolina); Lorraine Smith, Lake Pointe Elementary School (Texas); Diane Mentzer, Paramount Elementary School (Maryland); Missi Grove, Wynford School District (Ohio); Francis Thong, Hong Kong International School (Hong Kong); Gordon Dahlby, West Des Moines Community School District (Iowa); Leigh T. Ausband, Richland County School District Office (South Carolina); Ted Sakshaug, Wheatland-Chili Schools (New York); Alison James, Toowoomba Christian College (Australia); Camilla Gagliolo, Arlington Public Schools (Virginia); Ron Spicer, Affton School District (Missouri); Richard Archibald-Woodward, Ontario-Montclair School District (California); Sue Feldman, Newhall Elementary School (California); and Susan Hustad, International Elementary School #407 (California).

# *About the Author*

Prior to embarking on a career as an author and consultant, Susan Brooks-Young spent more than 23 years as a preK–8 teacher, site administrator, and technology specialist at a county office of education. Since 1986, she has written articles, columns, and reviews for a variety of education journals. She has published six books about technology for education leaders; they have received international attention. Susan focuses much of her energy on working with school administrators and their role in successfully implementing instructional technology programs. To that end, she works on a variety projects across the United States. Susan is also a regular speaker at national and international conferences.

When not on the road, Susan and her husband divide their time between Vancouver, British Columbia, and their farm on Lopez Island in Washington State.

# *Introduction*

*Education is the only business still debating the usefulness of technology. Schools remain unchanged for the most part, despite numerous reforms and increased investments in computers and networks.*

—Former U.S. Secretary of Education Rod Paige

Public education is one of the most successful institutions of the Industrial Age. We did a crackerjack job convincing students that a high school diploma was their ticket to a better-paying job, particularly following World War II. According to the National Center for Education Statistics just 95,000 students graduated from U.S. public *and* private high schools in 1900. One hundred years later, the number of public high school graduates alone was 2,809,000. A much smaller proportion of these students completed a college degree, but for much of the twentieth century, high school graduates had access to well-paid jobs in manufacturing and other industries.

Things are different today. Thanks to developments in technology, the world outside school walls has seen more change in one generation than in all previous generations put together. Outsourcing and offshoring has moved many manufacturing jobs overseas. Work is still available in the United States, but people need different kinds of skills to qualify for these jobs. For example, the U.S. Department of Labor makes forecasts about what jobs will see the greatest growth every decade. Each of the top 10 growth areas for this decade requires significant technology skills! In most cases, our schools are struggling to keep up with these changes.

Just as the one-room schoolhouse had to make way for a new model for education in industrial America, twenty-first-century educators must accept the fact that in order to prepare our students to be successful in a technology-infused global economy, we need to make some significant changes. Employers now expect that new hires will arrive with an expanded skill set that includes basic technology use. Where will these skills be learned, if we're not teaching them? Incorporating effective, regular use of technology as a tool for teaching and learning is imperative, if we want to stay on top of the game.

> Leadership could be considered the single most important aspect of effective school reform.
>
> —Robert J. Marzano

There was a time when most educators assumed that if teachers had access to technology, they would naturally incorporate its use into the instructional day. We know now that some teachers will make this shift, but most don't. Why? There are a number of reasons, but beginning in the mid-1990s, one critical roadblock was identified and then substantiated in multiple studies. This research clearly shows that administrative leadership has a direct impact on all successful school reform, including the quantity and quality of technology use in schools. Two well-known studies that include this finding are the Apple Classrooms of Tomorrow report written by SRI (www.apple.com/education/k12/leadership/acot/) and a report from SouthEast Initiatives Regional Technology in Education Consortium (SEIR♦TEC), *Lessons Learned: Factors Influencing the Effective Use of Technology for Teaching and Learning* (www.seirtec.org/publications/lessons.pdf). Each report points out that in those instances where administrators take steps to support technology integration programs, teachers and students are far more likely to engage in regular, appropriate use of technology than in schools where administrative leadership is lacking in this area. (For a more in-depth discussion of effective change in educators' use of technology, please refer to the final section of Chapter 12.)

In order to become effective technology leaders, aspiring and practicing administrators must engage in ongoing professional development. But many administrators aren't sure where to begin. The National Educational Technology Standards for Administrators (NETS■A), released in 2002, offer a comprehensive framework educational leaders can use to identify courses, workshops, and materials that will meet their needs for professional development in this area. The material in this book is designed to provide administrators, and other school leaders, with up-to-date information and resources that align with NETS■A. More information about the standards can be found at http://cnets.iste.org/administrators/.

The chapters in this book originally appeared between 2002 and 2005 as articles in two professional magazines published by the Peter Li Education Group: *Today's School* and *Today's Catholic Teacher*. Reader response was consistently positive, with many requests for permission to share articles in classes and meetings. However, the audience has been limited to subscribers of these two magazines and colleagues of those readers. This publication makes the material available to a much wider audience.

The articles have been reviewed and updated. To assist readers in using the readings as working tools, additional online resources are listed at the end of each chapter, and discussion questions have been added to encourage application of the material. Whether you're reading the book on your own, as part of a professional learning community, or as a text for a course, you will find practical information designed to increase your leadership skills.

The book is divided into four sections, each focusing on a different aspect of technology leadership. The sections are New Literacies, Engaging Teachers and Students, Providing a Reliable Infrastructure, and Legal and Social Concerns. Each chapter includes an introduction explaining why this topic is of importance to administrators, annotated lists of additional resources for further research, and discussion questions appropriate for use in personal reflection or with professional learning communities. While the chapters can be read sequentially, it's also possible to pick and choose just those that address a particular need.

Individual administrators can use these chapters for personal growth and reflection. They may also want to share chapters and resources with staff, using the discussion questions as a springboard for grade-level, departmental, or staff meeting discussions. Small groups of administrators who have formed a professional learning community can use the book in the same way. Professional development providers or course instructors may use the chapters and discussion questions as the foundation for class activities or projects.

# PART I

## *New Literacies*

The chapters in this section discuss new literacies for the twenty-first century, strategies for helping teachers incorporate these skills into instruction, and the role of library/media centers in addressing the expanded definitions of literacy.

# 1

# Integration Issues for Twenty-First-Century Teachers

Desktop computers began to appear in classrooms 25 years ago. Early adopters enthusiastically proclaimed that this technology would radically change educational practice. Today, there are schools where things are not "business as usual." However, this is the exception rather than the rule. Why are educators struggling with how to use technology in ways that actually do impact student performance? This chapter discusses critical factors in the quest to bring our schools into the twenty-first century, technologically speaking.

"I don't see that using technology has made any difference in how well my students perform." This comment was made recently during a workshop I was conducting for technology planning teams. Heads were nodding in agreement all around the room. It seemed to be one of those teachable moments, so we stopped what we were doing to discuss this

SOURCE: *Today's Catholic Teacher,* January/February 2005

comment. I asked for examples of the kinds of technology-supported instruction the participants offered. Several responded:

- "After they finish their other work, I let students play education games on the computer."
- "My students made a five-slide PowerPoint show for their science fair project using a template I made for them."
- "Students read a book and then take a quiz online."
- "We go to the computer lab and I let them look for Web sites; but usually by the time they find something, our lab time is over."

These comments are typical of the ways many teachers bring technology to their students. Nothing is inherently wrong with any of these activities as a starting point; however, in far too many instances, this is as far as a teacher is willing to go. If you consider each example carefully, you can see that the teacher has taken something s/he would have done anyway and simply automated it. For example, supplemental educational games have been used as time-fillers for decades. Now, instead of playing a board game, students play online. Science fair projects have moved from poster boards to PowerPoint slides, but the information is still presented in a linear fashion. Reading quizzes are taken online rather than on paper, but the comprehension-level questions haven't changed. Students who once might have spent their library time trying to find just the right print material now do the same thing using a search engine instead. The bottom line is that none of these activities is enhanced or made better through the use of technology. Doing the same old thing a little faster or a little more efficiently isn't going to change academic outcomes.

## NEW DEMANDS FOR EDUCATION

If we were still preparing students to function in a society where basic content literacy, getting to work on time, and following directions were usually enough to ensure successful adult lives, we might be able to settle for automation of instructional tasks. But the demands that will be placed on our students when they enter the workplace are much greater. Along with basic academic knowledge, our students must now be prepared to become lifelong learners who can manage large quantities of information, solve problems, think critically, work in teams, and use technology effectively. Technology tools can help teachers design activities that prepare students to deal with expanded workplace demands, but only if those teachers are willing to become more advanced technology users themselves and implement new teaching strategies. *Lesson Learned: Factors Influencing the Effective Use of Technology for Teaching and Learning,* a report published by the SouthEast Initiatives Regional Technology in

Education Consortium (SEIR ♦ TEC), states, "Effective use of technology requires changes in teaching; in turn, the adoption of a new teaching strategy can be a catalyst for technology integration."

The Apple Classrooms of Tomorrow research, published in the mid-1990s and available at www.apple.com/education/k12/leadership/acot/library.html, found that teachers go through several stages of use before they are fully ready to integrate the use of technology as a teaching tool. The activities described above all fall in the early stages of use. Teachers need specific professional development to move into the later stages, where increased student performance can be attributed to technology use. However, even with this training, additional factors can impede teachers in making effective use of technology in their classrooms. Lack of follow-up after training and continuing support thereafter are issues; so is the fact that most teachers view technology quite differently than their students view it.

## DIGITAL IMMIGRANTS AND DIGITAL NATIVES

### What's the Difference?

> dig·i·tal im·mi·grant *n*: A technology user, usually over the age of 30, who was not born into the digital world. Digital immigrants use technology, but often attempt to bring this use into a framework they finds comfort in; for example, they might print material accessed on the Internet before reading it.

> dig·i·tal na·tive *n*: A technology user under the age of 30, who was born into the digital world and is accustomed to receiving information very quickly. Digital natives are able to multitask, and they usually prefer to see graphics before text. They tend to be more comfortable working in a hyperlinked environment and when they receive frequent rewards or feedback.

One of the impediments to effective technology integration is the fact that most of the teachers in classrooms today did not grow up as technology users themselves. In 2001, consultant and author Marc Prensky coined the terms *digital immigrant* and *digital native.* If you are more than 30 years old, or had little opportunity to use technologies such as personal computers during your own childhood, you are a digital immigrant. You probably remember when cell phones were an oddity, when computer diskettes were 5¼" floppies, and when VHS tapes were high-end video technology.

In his article "Digital Natives, Digital Immigrants," Prensky writes that learning to use technology as an adult is akin to learning how to speak a new language at the same age. Although it's possible to become proficient in a new language after childhood, most adult learners will speak with an accent. The same is true with technology use. Digital immigrants can achieve proficiency with new technologies; however, most attempt to use these new tools within the framework of their own previous learning. This approach leads to accomplishing familiar tasks faster, but ignores those capabilities that would enable them to approach and complete these tasks in new ways. For example, a digital immigrant might use a handheld device to take notes at a meeting, but not know how to beam the notes to others at the end of the meeting, falling back on printing and distributing paper copies later. This behavior is the digital immigrant's "accent," and Prensky argues that it is this accent that causes educators, most of whom are still digital immigrants, to struggle with technology integration in the classroom.

Today's students are digital natives. They come to us with very different technology-related experiences, attitudes, and expectations than we had growing up because they were born into the digital age; they don't know anything different. Many of them have never seen a telephone with a dial, a cash register without scanning capability, or a manual adding machine. Recent surveys show that these children spend more time using the Internet than they do watching television, and that the age group experiencing the greatest increase in time spent online consists of two- to five-year-olds! Respondents also report that the place where they have the least opportunity to use technology is at school. In some cases this may be due in part to limited access; however, even in well-equipped schools technology use is often limited.

## WHEN DIGITAL IMMIGRANTS TEACH DIGITAL NATIVES

Even when students have adequate access to technology tools, teachers often insist that they draft an essay by hand before allowing them to use a word processor. Or students sit down at Internet-connected computers and then are forbidden to use the systems during the bulk of the lesson in an effort to ensure that they are on task. This tendency of digital immigrants to restrict students' use of technology, even when access is not an issue, is a major barrier to effective integration of technology in classrooms.

Teachers' common reaction to multitasking is a prime example. Digital immigrants tend to be fairly linear in their approach to work and prefer to complete one task before moving on to the next. Digital natives are accustomed to doing several things all at once, such as watching television, reviewing a Web site, taking notes, and instant-messaging friends. Based upon their own style of learning, digital immigrants often assume that multitasking students can't possibly be paying attention, and so their digital-immigrant teachers try to change this behavior. As a result, situations arise such as at one school where students were provided wireless mobile computing devices only to have the teachers prohibit use of the devices during most of the school day!

Technology use is no longer an optional part of life outside the classroom and should not be optional inside the classroom either. Students in the twenty-first century need daily equitable access to technology tools in their school environment, just as they have access to other staples for learning. And for students to make best use of the technology, teachers must be willing to think beyond their own experiences as students and to realize that instructional strategies designed 100 years ago to teach students to be good assembly-line workers are not appropriate in today's classrooms.

## THINKING OUTSIDE OF THE DIGITAL IMMIGRANT'S BOX

While we may not be able to anticipate everything our students will need to know in the future, we can teach them skills that will serve them well now and then. Teachers can take several steps to compensate for their technology accent. Below are some suggestions.

**Learn everything you can about twenty-first-century skills.** A number of Web sites address twenty-first-century skills and their impact on education. The Partnership for 21st Century Skills (www.21stcenturyskills.org) and the North Central Regional Educational Laboratory's enGauge (www .ncrel.org/engauge) Web sites—which feature reports, resources, and tools for teachers—are two good places to start.

**Don't settle for basic personal proficiency.** Become a lifelong learner yourself. Basic skills will help you automate; learning more advanced technology skills will help you see potential you didn't know existed. For example, simple PowerPoint slides are equivalent to overhead transparencies. More advanced features including hyperlinks, movies, or online collaboration capabilities open all sorts of possibilities for more effective classroom use of this program.

**Review sample lessons for ideas.** It's often helpful to look at examples of how other teachers are incorporating technology use into classroom instruction that supports twenty-first-century learning skills. Some Web sites that feature lessons and projects of this type include Marco Polo Teacher Resources (www.marcopolo-education.org/teacher/teacher_ index.aspx); ThinkQuest (www.thinkquest.org/), and the Handbook of Engaged Learning Projects (www-ed.fnal.gov/help/index.html).

**Turn to digital natives for ideas.** If you are uncomfortable about asking your own students to suggest new or better ways to design classroom projects, approach other digital natives you know. Talk to your own children, nieces and nephews, or neighbors. Ask them to describe projects that would be interesting and relevant to them and how technology could be used to enhance the learning experience from their point of view. Not only will they be happy to share their thoughts, but many will also be willing to show you how to use the technologies they describe.

Let's return to the examples given at the beginning of this chapter. How could these activities be expanded to enhance student learning? Instead of allowing students to play games, teach them to use tools such as Filamentality (http://www.filamentality.com/wired/fil/index.html) or TrackStar (http://trackstar.4teachers.org/trackstar/) to create and share their own activities based on academic content. Both sites allow teachers to design activities in which students respond to prompts or discussion questions. Forgo the comprehension level questions found in many online book quizzes and create your own using questions at higher levels of Bloom's taxonomy. Use the advanced capabilities of PowerPoint or another presentation program to encourage students to demonstrate connections in what they learned during their science fair project rather than as a basic reporting tool. And finally, to help students maximize the effectiveness of their use of online time, teach critical thinking skills for effective Internet searches as well as strategies for evaluating the quality of Web sites.

A major shift in thinking takes time. Begin slowly and build your repertoire of new skills and strategies. The problem doesn't lie in incremental change; the problem lies in little or no change at all.

## ADDITIONAL RESOURCES

In addition to the resources cited above, you can learn more by accessing these online resources:

Apple Computer, Inc., Digital Tools for Digital Kids: http://www.apple.com/education/digitalkids/. This site takes a look at who digital kids are and how they learn. Along with the information presented on each page, there are links to video commentary and articles about twenty-first-century learners.

"Digital Natives, Digital Immigrants" at Marc Prensky's Web site: http://www.marcprensky.com/writing/Prensky%20-%20Digital%20Natives,%20Digital%20Immigrants%20-%20Part1.pdf (2001). Marc Prensky's original article in which he describes digital immigrants and their impact on teaching and learning.

National Institute for Literacy and the Office of Vocational and Adult Education, Division of Adult Education and Literacy: http://worklink .coe.utk.edu/. Take a look at the needs of today's learners through the lens of adult education using links to research, news, and a Learning Activities Bank.

21st Century Literacies: http://www.filamentality.com/wired/ 21stcent/. Created to support the SBC/UCLA Initiatives for 21st Century Literacies project, this site offers a free, Web-based video called *e-literate* (http://www.kn.pacbell.com/media/ucla.html). There are also sample lesson plans for teaching *information, media, multicultural,* and *visual* literacy skills.

## QUESTIONS FOR DISCUSSION

1. What do you see as the critical issue in this chapter?

2. What are the differences between *digital immigrants* and *digital natives?*

3. Describe an example of a "digital accent" from your own experience or observation.

4. The chapter begins with several examples of classroom activities that are commonly automated today. What examples of automation have you seen in your school/district/region?

5. How do the expanded activities described at the end of the chapter differ from the earlier examples?

6. How might the information in this chapter impact technology use in your school/district/region? List your ideas.

7. What steps will you take to think outside the digital box?

# 2

---

# *Information Literacy*

Faculty and students at the School of Information Management and Systems at the University of California, Berkeley, conducted a study called *How Much Information? 2003.* The study tracked the amount of new information stored on paper, film, magnetic, and optical media, and showed that, worldwide, the amount of new information nearly doubled between 2000 and 2003. There is no sign that this growth will slow down any time soon. As a result, it is imperative that today's schools teach students how to deal with this deluge of information. But this will require changes in teaching strategies and curriculum, and school leaders will need to take the lead.

*Information literacy: the ability to access, evaluate, and use information effectively.*

—The Association of College and Research Libraries, 2000

At one point in history, being literate simply meant that a person could read and write. In some cases just the ability to sign one's name was enough to be considered literate. However, changes in societal needs along with increased access to information and a better-educated population led to broadened expectations about what literacy entailed, resulting in expanded definitions for the term.

---

SOURCE: *Today's School,* May/June 2002

Francis Bacon (1561–1626) said, "Knowledge is power," implying that people who possessed knowledge definitely had the edge over people who did not. Writers and philosophers grappled with the concept of widespread education during the Age of Enlightenment. Rousseau, Locke, and other eighteenth-century thinkers heavily influenced many of the nineteenth-century educators who helped lay the foundation for modern public education. So today, when I hear information literacy presented as though it's a relatively new development based upon technology use, or a separate curricular issue relegated to the realm of library/media specialists, I'm a bit skeptical. What is new is what educators now mean when they use the term *literacy*, which has been expanded to include skills for accessing, evaluating, and using information now available in new formats.

It's important that educators take some time to think about what they mean by information literacy. The concept encompasses so many different types of skills that educators need to come to an agreement about what the elements of information literacy are, how to construct a balanced approach to teaching skills, and who will be responsible for implementing this approach.

## CHANGING IDEAS ABOUT LITERACY

*A Nation at Risk: The Imperative for Educational Reform*, published in 1983 by the National Commission on Excellence in Education, provided the impetus to seriously question the structure of K–12 public education in the United States. Subsequent documents including *Educating Students to Think: The Role of the School Library Media Program* (1986, Jacqueline C. Mancall, Shirley L. Aaron, and Sue A. Walker), *Information Power: Guidelines for School Library Media Programs* (1988, American Library Association and Association for Educational Communications and Technology), and *Information Power: Building Partnerships for Learning* (1998, American Library Association and Association for Educational Communications and Technology) stressed the importance of school library/media centers in teaching students to become critical consumers of information. *What Work Requires of Schools*, the 1991 report of the Secretary's Commission on Achieving Necessary Skills (SCANS), identified primary literacy skills for the workforce of the future that far surpassed basic reading, writing, and arithmetic. The content of these reports, along with advances in technology during the last 10 to 15 years that make it possible for people to access what was a once unimaginable amount of information, bring a sense of urgency to changing how we view literacy.

Look again at the definition for information literacy at the start of this chapter. Think about what it actually says. The key words are: *access, evaluate,* and *use.* Now think about all the different information formats available to teachers and students: books, magazines, newspapers, periodicals, e-mail, television, radio, the Internet, software, movies, and video are just a few. All of these resources, along with others, contain valuable information that may or may not be available in another format. In order to have full access to information, students must not only have computer literacy skills, but also reading, numeric, media, and visual literacy skills as well. So in order for students to become "information literate," they must master a variety of skills that provide a foundation for finding information. In addition, once students have the skills that enable them to locate information, they need to understand how to evaluate the accuracy of the material and how to synthesize the information and put it to use.

## INFORMATION LITERACY STANDARDS

The American Association of School Librarians (AASL) identifies nine information literacy standards for students, clustered into three categories: information literacy, independent learning, and social responsibility. The purpose of the standards, which address not only accessing information but also how it is used, is to provide a framework for library and media specialists as they work with teachers, students, and other school community members in support of enabling students to become lifelong learners.

Are information literacy skills the basis for a separate curriculum that is confined to the school library, or are they part of a process that needs to be woven throughout instruction in all content areas? Despite the fact that much of the available literature emphasizes the role of the school library/media specialist in the development of information literacy skills, most research supports the notion that acquiring information literacy is an ongoing process. This does not negate the importance of the library or of the specialist. Instead, it supports the fact that library/media specialists' influence cannot begin and end at the library entrance. Library/media specialists must be active members of the school community, working collaboratively with administrators, teachers, students, and parents to help students achieve information literacy.

National and state content standards documents further support approaching the idea of information literacy as a process by incorporating standards into content. For example, the Standards for the English Language Arts, sponsored by the National Council of Teachers of English and the International Reading Association, discuss students gathering, evaluating, and synthesizing information from a variety of on- and off-line resources and developing the ability to use language for a variety of purposes. California's Reading Literacy Performance Standards emphasize not only being able to read and understand text, but also being able to synthesize information and apply it in new settings.

# INFORMATION LITERACY MODELS

As early as 1993, AASL recommended that the teaching of information literacy skills be infused throughout the curriculum, identifying seven steps to be included in programs that develop information literacy skills. The steps are: define the need for information, initiate the search strategy, locate the resources, assess and comprehend the information, interpret the information, communicate the information, and evaluate the product and process. There are now several models for teaching information literacy. The Stripling/Pitts Model, the Kuhlthau Search Process Model, and the Pappas/Tepe Pathways to Knowledge Information Skills Model are examples. It's not practical to discuss all the different models here, so I've chosen to highlight two others—the Big6 and Super3 models—developed by Michael Eisenberg and Robert Berkowitz.

### The Big6 and Super3 Models

Like the steps recommended by AASL, the Big6 model looks at the entire process of research and provides a natural approach to tackling information literacy. Although they originally designed it for use as a library skills curriculum, its creators, Mike Eisenberg and Bob Berkowitz, soon realized that the approach worked across the curriculum in any situation where students are asked to access, evaluate, and use information. There are six identified stages in this approach:

1. **Task definition**—Students identify the problem or task and the information they will need to solve the problem or complete the task.

2. **Information seeking strategies**—Students use these to brainstorm possible information resources and then identify those that they believe will be the best sources for the particular task.

3. **Location and access**—Students find the resources and then use them to locate the information within the resources.

4. **Use of information**—Students review the information source and find the specific information they need.

5. **Synthesis**—The information from multiple sources is organized and presented.

6. **Evaluation**—Both the final product and the process used are reviewed and evaluated.

Even young children are able to use a modified approach to this model.

The Super3 enables primary students to exercise beginning skills through the following three steps:

1.  **Plan**—Help students think about the task before beginning it. Talk with them about what they are being asked to do and how they might accomplish it.

2.  **Do**—Complete the task.

3.  **Review**—Discuss both the final product and the process students used to create the product. Ask them to explain their thinking as they planned and completed the work.

The Big6 Web site features articles discussing the transfer of information literacy skills from classroom settings to real-world situations and provides examples of ways to integrate information literacy skills across the curriculum. You can learn more about the Big6 and Super3, review lesson plans, and access various tools by visiting www.big6.com/index.php.

## HOW DOES THIS AFFECT LEARNING?

Teaching information literacy is a group effort. In order for students to become critical consumers of information, they need assistance from teachers, library/media specialists, administrators, and their parents. Educators must have basic information literacy skills themselves, including the prerequisite reading, computer, visual, media, and numeric skills. It is no longer optional for an educator to choose not to develop skills in one or more of these areas such as computer literacy, or to take the viewpoint that modeling and teaching these skills are the responsibility of another grade level or department. Every adult who works with students needs to teach these skills when the need arises.

### Teachers

Teachers have opportunities to model their own information literacy skills for students throughout the school day. They also must consciously present information literacy skills to students by using vocabulary that relates to the process and by discussing the various steps of the process as students are engaged in learning. Every lesson taught every day provides opportunities to help students increase their literacy skills and understand the context of what they are doing. In addition, teachers can

- Make a variety of resources available to students in the classroom and through visits to the library
- Collaborate with the school's library/media specialist to develop projects that require students to use information literacy skills

- Encourage parents to make print and other resources available at home and to actively discuss school and homework with their children
- Participate in professional development activities designed to strengthen their own information literacy skills

## Library/Media Specialists

Library/media specialists help students by teaching them about the resources the library offers and how to use them. Every visit to the library is an opportunity for children to improve their skills in finding, evaluating, and using information. Library/media specialists should actively engage students in this process. They also support student learning by

- Working collaboratively with teachers to plan lessons and deliver instruction
- Offering training to teachers to assist them in making better use of library resources both at school and within the community
- Providing workshops for parents who want to learn more about information literacy skills in order to help their children, and also to encourage parents to serve as library volunteers
- Working with school administrators to develop a library/media center master plan that includes a working budget for acquisitions
- Participating on school site committees
- Exploring ways to extend library hours on-site or through partnerships with public libraries

## School Administrators

Visionary leaders model the importance of information literacy by making it a site priority. You can do this by

- Using classroom observations to identify how teachers are incorporating information literacy skills into lessons
- Modeling the use of various information sources
- Working with staff to develop a master plan for the library/media center that includes a reasonable budget
- Visiting the school library regularly and evaluating the program's effect on student learning
- Exploring ways to make the library more accessible to students and parents
- Supporting special programs that spotlight various kinds of literacy
- Funding professional development for staff and parents

An online resource you may find helpful is *School Library Program: A Handbook for School Administrators*, located at www.upei.ca/~fac_ed/

projects/handbook/index.htm. Library science students at the University of Prince Edward Island in Canada developed this handbook.

## Parents

Parents need to reinforce the importance of education and information literacy at home as well. Here are some simple things they can do:

- Attend meetings and workshops sponsored by the school to learn how to assist children with homework
- Volunteer to help in classrooms or in the library
- Ask questions about what children are doing at school
- Monitor the television programs and movies that children watch and talk with them about what they see
- Provide books and other print material at home

ERIC (Educational Resources Information Center) offers a free online brochure for parents entitled "What Should Parents Know About Information Literacy?" available at www.libraryinstruction.com/parents .html. Two additional online resources for parents are the Families Connect Web site, designed for parents and students to use together to access resources, articles, online tutorials, and tips (www.ala.org/ala/ aasl/schlibrariesandyou/parentsandcomm/parents.htm); and KidsClick! Worlds of Web Searching (www.rcls.org/wows/), which provides nine activities parents can use with their children to help them learn effective Web searching skills.

## Students

Students must also take responsibility for their own learning. Some approaches they may take include

- Using various literacy skills including those of reading, numeric, computer, media, and visual literacy
- Avoiding dependence upon one type of information source—yes, the Internet may be easiest to access, but it's not always the best or most accurate source of information
- Working in study groups to learn how to be good team members and to explore various ways to use and share information

Students may also want to visit the American Association of School Librarians' KC Tools Web site at www.ala.org/ala/aasl/schlibrariesand you/k12students/aaslkctools.htm. This site offers a research toolbox with supporting links to additional resources.

## CONCLUSION

One of the most critical elements of your approach to information literacy instruction will be balance. Library/media specialists across the country report that many students are so enamored with the Internet and online databases today that they resist using other resources when gathering information. Technology skills are important and necessary, but students need to be taught how to find and use other information resources as well. Being truly information literate means being able to identify, access, evaluate, and use the best resources for the task at hand, regardless of format.

## ADDITIONAL RESOURCES

In addition to the resources cited above, you can learn more by accessing these online resources:

"The Research Cycle," in *From Now On, The Educational Technology Journal*, Vol. 9, No. 4: http://questioning.org/rcycle.html (December 1999). Jamie McKenzie's seven-step research model is described here.

*Information Literacy:* http://kcsos.kern.org/tlc_resources/stories/ story Reader$26. This is an e-book about information literacy and education.

National Forum on Information Literacy: http://www.infolit.org/. Created in 1989, this forum examines the role of information in modern lives and supports international information literacy projects.

NoodleTools: http://www.noodletools.com/. This site offers a suite of free and subscription tools for students and teachers to use when conducting research.

Information Literacy: http://www.kn.sbc.com/wired/21stcent/ information.html#imgraph. This Web site features K–12 information literacy lesson plans originally developed by teachers at the Seeds University Elementary School, UCLA.

## QUESTIONS FOR DISCUSSION

1.  Define information literacy.

2.  How does the notion of information literacy change the traditional definition of literacy?

3.  Explain how information literacy skills are currently taught in your school/district.

4.  Review the stages of the Big6 and Super3 models for teaching information literacy. Give an example of how staff in your school/district could use these models.

5.  The chapter states that teaching information literacy is a group effort. What groups are identified? How would you enlist the aid of these same groups at your school/district?

6.  Review the suggested action steps for each group that should take part in teaching information literacy. What additional action steps would you recommend? What action steps would you not recommend?

7.  Most state and national academic standards now reference information literacy skills such as finding and evaluating resources, synthesizing resources, sharing information, etc. How are information literacy skills addressed in your state's academic standards for language arts, social science, science, or mathematics?

$$3$$

# *Visual Literacy*

## *Taking Things at Face Value*

With the current information explosion, experts argue that twenty-first-century educators must give up the Industrial Age notion that a good education consists of imparting a finite body of knowledge that can be covered through a standard-ized curriculum. This does not mean that teachers should abandon content; however, it does mean that educators also need to incorporate instruction that addresses how students can process all this information. In a society whose members are inundated with images, visual literacy is an increasingly important skill for students to master.

In late April 2003, a photo depicting a British soldier near Basra direct-ing a group of civilians away from possible Iraqi fire appeared on the front page of the *Los Angeles Times*. Close examination of the photo showed that several of the civilians appeared more than once! The photographer, who was fired, admitted he had taken two pictures and later combined them into one image to improve the composition of the shot.

SOURCE: *Today's Catholic Teacher*, January/February 2004

Nationally known food and drink products are casually placed on the set of a highly rated television program. Although no specific mention is made of these items, popular actors are seen consuming several of the products during a scene. Called *product placement,* this is actually an advertising strategy, and it's likely that the manufacturer paid the production company for the products' appearance.

A three-dimensional graph printed in a magazine shows Dow Jones averages over a period of time, and seems to suggest that the economy is improving significantly. However, a closer look reveals that the scale of the X axis has been manipulated so that very small gains appear to be monumental. Viewers who simply skim the graphic are left with the impression that the economy is strongly on the upswing.

As these examples demonstrate, children growing up in today's information society need more than the basic three Rs to understand the world around them. The North Central Regional Educational Laboratory (NCREL) hosts a comprehensive area on its Web site devoted entirely to twenty-first-century literacy skills, those skills today's students need to be successful (www.ncrel.org/engauge/skills/skills.htm). Skills are organized into four categories: digital-age literacy, inventive thinking, effective communication, and high productivity. According to NCREL, in addition to the three Rs students must now develop digital-age literacy skills in seven additional areas! This column focuses on one of these digital-age literacy skill areas: visual literacy. In addition to defining visual literacy, we'll look at how teachers can use technology to help students develop visual literacy skills.

## WHAT IS VISUAL LITERACY?

Our culture relies heavily on visuals as sources of information. We are bombarded with images through television, movies, newspapers, magazines, the Internet, and billboards. The NCREL site defines visual literacy as " . . . the ability to interpret, use, appreciate, and create images and video using both conventional and 21st century media in ways that advance thinking, decision making, communication, and learning." In order to be fully visually literate, students must be able not only to make sense out of what they see, but also to understand how images are created and manipulated to elicit particular responses. Therefore, a comprehensive approach to teaching visual literacy includes not only asking students to interpret images created by others, but also to create images to convey specific messages. Fortunately, the technology tools needed to support this instruction are commonly found in schools today or are inexpensive enough to be obtained easily. Computers with Internet access and application software, digital cameras, and scanners can all be used in teaching visual literacy skills.

## COMPUTERS WITH INTERNET
## ACCESS AND APPLICATION SOFTWARE

The Internet offers many resources for teachers who wish to develop lessons teaching students to interpret visual images. The Library of Congress Web site hosts the American Memory Collection at http://memory.loc.gov/ammem/. In addition to the digital collections, a teachers' area explains how educators can access images and offers lesson plan ideas. Similar resources include the National Gallery of Art at www.nga.gov, and the Smithsonian at www.si.edu. Students can also hone their interpretive visual literacy skills by regularly using a rubric to evaluate the Web pages they visit for other class assignments.

Application software can be used as a basis for lessons in which students create and manipulate their own images. Spreadsheet programs such as Excel enable students to generate a variety of charts and graphs and manipulate the elements to emphasize or minimize statistics reported graphically. Word processors, presentation programs, and desktop publishing tools (e.g., Word, PowerPoint, and Publisher) can include visuals designed to make specific points or elicit certain responses from viewers. Multimedia programs (e.g., FrontPage, DreamWeaver, or Photoshop) can be used to build Web sites or manipulate digitized images accessed online. Concept mapping programs such as Inspiration help students organize their thoughts graphically.

For additional resources to help with the use of computers, the Internet, and software to teach visual literacy, visit the Word to Image: Image to Word Web site at http://t3.preservice.org/T0211900/hotlist.html or try the Visual Literacy lessons at www.kn.pacbell.com/wired/ 21stcent/visual.html.

## DIGITAL CAMERAS

Many teachers who are otherwise technology-shy readily adopt the use of digital cameras, along with a computer and printer, in their classrooms. There are several reasons for this. First, the technology is familiar and easy to learn; most people have used a camera and can transfer this skill to the new technology. Second, digital cameras are now relatively inexpensive, both initially and in the long run. Prices have fallen quickly, and it's possible to pick up a decent camera for $300 or less. There are also products such as Jam Cams which are perfectly good for most student use and run as little as $30 to $50. And although there are costs for paper, printing, and storage (e.g., CDs for burning images) it's not necessary to buy film or pay for processing, and you have instant access to the pictures you take. Finally, digital cameras are excellent tools for recording events and for creative approaches to instruction, making them a natural tool for teaching visual literacy. Teachers can use the cameras to create images for students to analyze, and students can create their own images to communicate concepts to viewers.

If you're not already using a digital camera at school, think about how you would use this technology yourself and how you'd like students to use a camera to enhance the curriculum. While you might initially use the camera to record classroom events or activities and share these moments with parents through a newsletter or classroom Web site, don't confine yourself to this simple application. Take time to learn more about visual literacy and how using a digital camera can help your students develop skills in this area. Visit "Visual Literary Activities" at the Picture This site (www.museumca .org/picturethis/visual.html) and "Teaching with Digital Cameras" at the Tech4Learning site (www.tech4learning.com/services/teachingwithdigital-cameras.htm) for background information and ideas, and then brainstorm ideas of your own. For example, you might decide to take photos of interesting people, places, or things for students to use as writing prompts, or to take series of photos for student exercises in sequencing. You may want students to take photos that illustrate a concept in math, such as geometric shapes or examples of the Fibonacci number sequence in nature. You might also ask students to parody a well-known image, identifying and incorporating the elements of a famous photo or other graphic that make it memorable.

Once you've identified how you want to use a camera, you're ready to do some research to select the right camera. You'll have many to choose from. Popular manufacturers of digital cameras include Kodak (www .kodak.com), Olympus (www.olympusamerica.com), Sony (www.sony .com), Toshiba (www.toshiba.com), Canon (www.canon.com), and Casio (www.casio.com). The Short Courses Publishing Company Web site offers the free *Short Course in Choosing a Digital Camera* (www.shortcourses.com/ choosing/contents.htm). This e-book explains different types of digital cameras, current features and capabilities of digital cameras, and how digital cameras work. With this short course under your belt, you will find the suggestions in "What to Look for in a Digital Camera" very helpful (http:// reviews.cnet.com/4520-6501_7-5020667-1.html). This brief piece explains the specifications that will really matter when you narrow your choices for purchase. You will also want to read reviews of various cameras. The *Digital Photography Review* Web site can help here. Go to www.dpreview.com/; then click on Reviews, which takes you to an extensive list of current reviews of digital cameras by most major manufacturers.

As you and your students hone your photography skills, you may want to explore additional uses for your camera. There are a number of Internet sites devoted to using digital cameras in classrooms that offer ideas and lesson plans. Here are a few:

- **1001 Uses for a Digital Camera:** http://pegasus.cc.ucf.edu/~ ucfcasio/qvuses.htm
- **Going Digital in the Classroom:** http://www.forsyth.k12.ga.us/ sbeck/digital/goingdigital.htm
- **Teacher to Teacher:** http://www.brunswick.k12.me.us/lon/lonlinks/ digicam/teacher/home.html

Another possible use is photo editing. While your digital camera will come with computer software that allows you to do some basic editing, you may need to purchase a program such as Adobe Photoshop to do more sophisticated altering of photographs.

## SCANNERS

While not as popular as digital cameras, scanners also have a place in teaching visual literacy. Scanners are devices that connect to a computer and then read text or images and convert them into a digitized format that can be saved as a file, viewed on the monitor screen, and manipulated using software. Scanners are useful for digitizing photographs taken with film, student work such as drawings or handwritten documents, illustrations in books—basically, anything on paper. There are several types of scanners to choose from, but flatbed scanners, which resemble photocopying machines in both appearance and function, are most commonly used in schools. *PC World* magazine has posted a comprehensive, easy-to-understand guide called "How to Buy a Scanner" that can be accessed at www.pcworld.com/howto/bguide/0,guid,10,page,1,00.asp. The guide includes an explanation of specifications and offers shopping tips. Well-known manufacturers include Canon (www.canon.com), Epson (www.epson.com), and Hewlett-Packard (www.hewlettpackard.com).

In addition to digitizing images for use in visual literacy lessons, a popular use of scanners is the development of electronic portfolios for students and teachers. There are several Internet sites that offer suggestions for using scanners to build electronic portfolios such as Electronic Portfolios at www.essdack.org/port/.

## IMPORTANT REMINDERS

Don't forget about copyright and privacy when working with digital images. Chapter 20, "Copyright and Technology Use in the Classroom," covers this issue, and the text of this chapter is also available online at www.peterli.com/archive/tct/466.shtm. Review the four questions there for fair use of copyrighted material in the classroom. Since you may be working with images that include students, you also need to be familiar with your school's acceptable use policy along with other policies that address posting student work and likenesses on the Web.

Once you and your students are attuned to viewing graphics critically, you'll be amazed at the number of images you no longer take at face value. Don't miss the opportunity to expand this new awareness to discussions of the ethics of image manipulation. Your students will become prepared to make wise choices as learners and consumers.

## ADDITIONAL RESOURCES

In addition to the resources cited above, you can learn more by accessing these online resources:

Digital Cameras in Education: http://www.drscavanaugh.org/digital camera/. Information about digital cameras and suggestions for how they can be used in classrooms.

International Visual Literacy Association: http://www.ivla.org/. This organization provides a forum for educators, researchers, and artists who are interested in exchanging information about visual literacy.

Kodak Lesson Plans: http://www.kodak.com/US/en/digital/edu/ lessonPlans/. Lesson plans for using digital cameras and teacher guides organized by subject area and grade level.

Digital Cameras Enhance Education: http://members.ozemail .com.au/~cumulus/digcam.htm. Extensive information about using digital cameras in classrooms.

Visual Literacy K–8: http://k-8visual.info/. Updated monthly, this site offers materials and ideas for K–8 classrooms.

## QUESTIONS FOR DISCUSSION

1. Define visual literacy.

2. How does visual literacy differ from information literacy?

3. Based upon your own experience or observation, give an example of how visual images are used to elicit a response from a viewer,

4. How visually literate are students in your school/district? Explain.

5. Where does visual literacy fit into the instructional day? Give examples.

6. How might the information in this column impact instruction in your school/district? List your ideas.

# 4

# *Library/Media Centers*

## *Strategy for Improved Student Performance*

Benjamin Franklin and fellow members of the Leather Apron Club (a group of printers) established the first public lending library in the American colonies in 1731. By the late nineteenth century, public libraries were also serving public schools, which were often built near the local library. Educators recognized the importance of on-site libraries, and during the early twentieth century, secondary schools began establishing their own libraries, which also became home to growing media collections following World War II. Today, well-designed school libraries provide access to a variety of modern technologies, and the school librarians who run them work closely with teachers to provide instruction in twenty-first-century literacy skills to increase student achievement.

Think back to your own school library experiences as a student. Chances are when you were very young, the library was a place your class visited to hear the librarian read a story, and then you would check out books. As you grew older, teachers may have taken the class or sent groups

SOURCE: *Today's School*, January 2002

of students to do research for a project or term paper. You probably could not depend upon most school libraries to have all the materials you needed and so you visited the public library as well. Most likely, interactions with the school librarian were limited to the activities described above.

Today, taking advantage of technologies that provide for automation and improved communication, many school libraries are being transformed into library/media centers (LMCs) where students and teachers have access to materials in both traditional and electronic (Internet and software) formats. In addition to the collection housed on-site, patrons may be able to obtain materials at another school's library or from local public libraries through electronic catalogs. Teachers may be able to check on the availability of library materials through the school network without leaving their classrooms. The role of the librarian is changing as well, so much so that many are now called *library media specialists* (LMSs). This new specialist takes an active role in collaborating with teachers on lesson planning, teaching skills to students, participating on school committees, and making curricular decisions.

What is the impetus for this change, and how might it impact your own school library?

## RESEARCH ABOUT THE IMPACT OF SCHOOL LIBRARY/MEDIA CENTERS

Independent studies conducted in Alaska, Colorado, and Pennsylvania between 1998 and 2000 all found that students who have access to a robust LMC program perform better on standardized tests of academic achievement than their counterparts who do not have access to such a program. These findings held true across the grade levels included in the studies, regardless of widely varied socioeconomic factors.

What constitutes a robust LMC program? According to the authors of "Dick and Jane Go to the Head of the Class," published in the online *School Library Journal* (April 2000, http://schoollibraryjournal.com), a program on this scale features, "a full-time library media specialist, support staff, and a strong computer network (one that connects the library's resources to classrooms and labs)." This level of staffing and communication allows for several things to happen. First, and most importantly, library staff has time to collaborate with teachers on lesson-plan development and to teach information literacy skills to students when they visit the library. Staff also has time to offer professional development to teachers on a consistent basis. All three studies show a direct correlation between these activities and increased student performance. Second, additional staff allows library hours to be extended to provide additional opportunities for students and teachers to take advantage of the services offered. Finally, expanded access to information in the library and online through a computer network encourages teachers and students to make better and more frequent use of materials.

Another important factor is the level of involvement the library media specialist has with school operation overall and in developing partnerships with local public libraries. Although neither of these directly impacts student achievement when viewed in isolation, increased involvement with school staff and the community leads to better developed collaboration with these groups, which does have a proven effect on student achievement.

With accountability and student performance as high priorities, the results of these studies are important to educators and parents. While an enhanced LMC program is not the only solution, nor is it a quick fix, it is certainly one strategy that bears close examination.

## THE DIFFERENCE BETWEEN A LIBRARY AND A LIBRARY/MEDIA CENTER

You may be wondering what an LMC looks like and how it differs from a traditional library. At one time a library could be defined as a place that housed a collection of books, records, and films, and a librarian's role was to provide access to items in the collection. Today an LMC offers much more. It is a place where students and teachers can find information through a variety of resources to grapple with curriculum-based real-world issues. The librarian's role has shifted from curator to teacher of information literacy. Students and teachers who possess strong information literacy skills are able to access the information they need quickly, evaluate that information critically, and use the information to communicate new learning.

The physical design of LMCs is also different from that of the traditional library. Rather than one large room with bookshelves and reading tables, LMCs typically offer various areas for different kinds of work. You will find a center devoted to research and reading that houses print material accessed through an online catalog as well as Internet access that provides both research opportunities and an avenue to local and distant library collections. There may be another area where students are able to work together on projects; talking is encouraged and workspace is provided along with access to various multimedia tools. A computer lab for teaching literacy skills is also available. Here students learn how to conduct effective Internet searches, evaluate the material they find, and organize it to communicate what they have learned. A place where students can read for pleasure or browse periodicals and paperbacks for informal reading experiences is also included. The possibilities for reconfiguration are varied and exciting.

# HOW TECHNOLOGY SUPPORTS
# THE LIBRARY/MEDIA CENTER

## Automation

Many school librarians take the first step toward a technology-supported LMC program through automation of the current collection. Bar coding items and entering the data is time consuming, but the benefits become readily apparent. In addition to ready access to all items housed at one site, it becomes possible to create a unified catalog of all materials in the school district. While librarians often choose to run parallel systems (both paper and online) until all the bugs are worked out, most abandon paper systems as their comfort level with the automated system increases. There is an almost immediate savings in time for routine procedures such as managing circulation, tracking overdue materials, and updating the materials catalog. Time not spent in management becomes time available to spend with teachers and students. Most automation systems also permit school libraries to interface with other library systems and the Internet as well.

A number of publishers offer library automation programs. Some well known companies include Follett Software Company (www.fsc.follett .com), SirsiDynix Corporation (www.sirsi.com), CASPR Library Systems, (www.caspr.com), Sagebrush Corporation (www.sagebrushcorp.com), and COMPanion Corporation (www.goalexandria.com).

## Information Literacy

Think back to the elements of information literacy mentioned above. People who possess these literacy skills know how to find information, evaluate its merit, and communicate what they have learned. While use of electronic information is an important part of this skill set, it does not preclude the use of print material. A complete LMC offers access to information in all formats, as the following example demonstrates.

A high school English teacher assigns a project about theater in Shakespeare's time. Students are asked to work in groups to study various aspects of theatrical production: physical performance space and settings, costuming, props, casting, choice of scripts, directing, and performance techniques. First, the teacher meets with the LMS to develop a unit of instruction. The LMS contributes instruction on information literacy skills and knowledge about available electronic and print resources.

Students conduct Internet searches based on the techniques taught by the LMS. They gather information and meet with their teacher to discuss and evaluate its merit and to determine where additional research is needed. The LMS then works with the students to help them find resources that offer more in-depth information. After conducting additional research, students again meet with the teacher to review their new research and plan how this information will be presented to communicate new learning. Information may be organized using a program called Inspiration (www.inspiration.com) or the outlining feature of a word processor.

Numerous reporting options are available to students. Some may decide to write a traditional research-based paper using a word processing program. In this case, the library media specialist may show students how to develop a bibliography and use a specified format for the paper. Others may decide to create multimedia presentations using software such as HyperStudio (www.hyperstudio.com/) or PowerPoint (www.microsoft.com/office/). LMC support staff members are available to assist students in using multimedia software to create their presentations. When the projects are complete, student groups present their projects to the rest of the class to demonstrate their new learning.

## CONCLUSION

Current research clearly establishes the positive impact a LMC has on student performance. In a site-based management setting, the school staff should consider this research, review the existing library program, and identify ways the program can be improved or expanded to better meet student and teacher needs. It may be found that the additional cost of an up-to-date LMC can be leveraged to reduce the cost of remediation programs, resulting in improved student performance and self-esteem as well as a balanced budget. Making regular visits to the American Association of School Librarians Web site at www.ala.org will help you stay informed on additional research and trends in this important area.

## ADDITIONAL RESOURCES

In addition to the resources cited above, you can learn more by accessing these online resources:

American Association of School Librarians: http://www.ala.org/aaslhome/Template.cfm?Section=aasl. AASL supports leadership in school LMC programs. The site offers publications and professional tools for library media specialists.

Center for International Scholarship in School Libraries: http://cissl.scils.rutgers.edu/. This organization focuses on developing and sharing research to improve school libraries worldwide.

Library Research Service: http://www.lrs.org/index.asp. The mission of LRS is to provide research about libraries. The School link takes you to a variety of resources including school library statistics and impact studies.

National Center for Education Statistics: http://nces.ed.gov/surveys/libraries/. This URL takes you directly to the Library Statistics page. The School Libraries link leads to publications and surveys.

Resources for School Librarians: http://www.sldirectory.com/index .html. Maintained by a retired school librarian, this site provides links to resources for learning and teaching, information access, technology, and more.

## QUESTIONS FOR DISCUSSION

1. Describe the LMC program that currently exists in your school/district.

2. Explain methods used by your LMS to collaborate with teachers.

3. Describe your school/district curriculum for teaching information literacy skills.

4. Who currently teaches information literacy skills at your school/district? Give examples of how these skills are addressed.

5. How is technology used to enhance instruction in information literacy?

6. Based upon the information provided in this chapter, what are the strengths and weaknesses of the current program in your school/district?

7. What steps could be taken to enhance your current LMC program?

# Don't Limit the Value of the Library/Media Center

Educators often fail to recognize the contributions a well-run, professional library/ media center can make to increasing student achievement. With growing pressure to provide instruction in twenty-first-century literacy skills, the LMS needs to play an even greater role in the overall instructional program. But there are several common barriers that impede effective use of the LMC. Read this chapter to learn more about current practices that end up becoming stumbling blocks, and how to avoid (or correct) them.

Our students must master skills far beyond those of traditional literacy if they are to become successful global citizens. Twenty-first-century skills include the ability to use technology effectively; to find, evaluate, and synthesize increasing quantities of information; to critically view various types of media; and to become increasingly sensitive to cultural similarities and differences.

SOURCE: *Today's School*, January/February 2005

Teachers often need assistance in providing instruction in these new skills, and many educators struggle with how to strike a balance between covering mandated academic content and incorporating instruction in twenty-first-century skills. Yet most schools have a resource in place that can provide support in these areas and offer ongoing services to students. This resource is the library/media center (LMC). But many schools have made only limited progress in fully integrating use of the LMC into a school's instructional program.

I recently engaged in an online exchange with administrators and library/media specialists (LMSs) across the country. The discussion focused on existing practices that unintentionally create barriers and discourage schools from fully integrating use of the LMC into the instructional program. Three of these practices seemed to be prevalent: managing personnel costs by staffing the LMC with aides or clerks rather than credentialed specialists, use of the LMC to provide prep time for teachers, and overreliance on computer-based read-and-quiz programs to promote student reading. Let's take a closer look at these challenges and some possible solutions.

## MANAGING PERSONNEL COSTS

It's not unusual for secondary schools to hire at least one part-time, fully credentialed LMS. However, due to the cost involved and the lack of credentialed LMSs, elementary schools often hire aides or clerks who have little or no formal training beyond how to manage the collection. While this may keep books circulating and expose students to basic library-use skills, in-depth instruction related to twenty-first-century skills does not occur without specific planning.

Hiring a full-time LMS at one elementary site may not be an option, particularly if the budget is tight. In these instances, it's important that site administrators carefully consider their alternatives. Perhaps two or three schools can work together to split funding for a shared LMS and still provide daily on-site support through aides or clerks. One discussion participant described a pilot program in her district where the district and elementary sites have arranged to provide one credentialed LMS each to clusters of two or three schools, along with one trained LMC aide per school. Each LMS teaches twenty-first-century skills at assigned sites and also works with the aides to ensure program continuity, increasing the quality of programs offered to teachers and students.

When additional staffing isn't an option, consider an intensive training program for existing employees. Ongoing professional development will make a difference. A small district in central California has chosen this route. A credentialed LMS oversees the district program and trains on-site aides in how to teach information literacy skills using a district-adopted program. While there are drawbacks, the level of instruction taking place in each LMC has increased. You can find one model for skill development on a Web page developed by Dr. Lesley Farmer and hosted by California State University, Long Beach. This page features information literacy activities for students and teachers using streaming video and linked resources and may be accessed at www.csulb.edu/~lfarmer/infolitwebstyle.htm.

## PROVIDING PREP TIME FOR TEACHERS

Teachers need time to reflect and plan. High schools and middle schools build this preparation time into the master schedule. This is not so easy to accomplish on elementary campuses where teachers usually work in self-contained classrooms. It is increasingly common for these teachers to be given a prep time when their students visit the library. Collaborative activities, where library staff regularly share resources with teachers or coplan and teach lessons that infuse academic content with twenty-first-century learning skills, are a critical element in meeting the needs of students. One difficulty with using the LMC to provide teacher prep time is that it can hamper teacher/library staff collaboration. Even in situations where teachers and staff make time to plan activities together, the teacher's absence during the LMC visit often leads students to assume that what transpires there is not really connected to the classroom. And when teachers and library staff have not collaborated, there usually is a disconnect. In worst-case situations, visits to the LMC become nothing more than a time for students to hear a story and check out books that have little or no relationship to what's happening in the classroom.

What can be done to improve this situation? Provide professional development for teachers and library staff, focusing on the benefits of collaboration and strategies for effective planning. Include the LMS in staff meetings and discussions about curriculum. When appropriate, ask the LMS to provide short in-service trainings to teachers about new literacies and the LMC. Encourage staff to share ideas through a Web page or weblog where resources, lesson plans, or projects may be posted. The Greece Athena Media Center (www.greece.k12.ny.us/ath/library) is one example of how this can be accomplished. E-mail exchanges can also be useful when planning activities for class visits.

Whenever possible, teachers should accompany their students to the LMC and take an active role in instruction while there. Several administrators and LMC staff suggested that flexible scheduling is conducive to collaborative planning and effective instructional use of the LMC. This is because teachers are asked to meet with LMC staff to plan student activities as a prerequisite for scheduling a visit. If prep time and the LMC schedule are tied together, flexible scheduling and teacher presence may be difficult to arrange. In this case, regular communication and preplanning become more critical in order for the LMC staff to leverage this time to achieve maximum instructional benefits.

## RELUCTANT READERS

In order to encourage students to read, many schools have implemented computer-based read-and-quiz programs. Students read a book from a list of titles included in the program and then earn points by passing a computer-based quiz that tests basic knowledge and comprehension. Quiz points are often used to award prizes or grades. Most of these programs offer quizzes for thousands of titles across grade levels and also allow users to create their own quizzes and make adjustments to the points that are awarded.

In the short term, circulation numbers rise and collections grow as school staff and parents focus on promoting reading. Teachers appreciate the reporting capabilities of the software, which enable them to track students' quiz scores. However, when these programs become the driving force behind a school's supplemental reading program there are also unintended, less positive consequences.

For example, in some LMCs, books from the lists are displayed in a separate area. Students no longer need to use the catalog system to find the books that are worth points and virtually ignore the materials in the rest of the LMC. Many times students are required to earn a fixed number of points reading titles from the approved lists before being per-mitted to read books off the list for credit. Less technology-proficient teachers and LMC staff often rely on the automated quiz system as the predominant use of technology in the classroom or library. And students in classrooms where the teacher depends exclusively upon the electronic quizzes for feedback have fewer opportunities to explore their reading in depth.

Computer-based read-and-quiz programs can be a part of an overall literacy program, but should not become its sole focus. One creative approach to encouraging students to read more is the Reading Olympics staged annually in Chester County, Pennsylvania. Schools form teams of students who collaboratively read 40–50 books and then come together to participate in a competition focused on the books' content. Visit http://readingolympics.cciu.org to learn more.

LMCs can (and should) be an indispensable resource for increasing students' academic performance and in the development of twenty-first-century learning skills. In order for this to happen, we need to change our thinking about the purpose of the LMC and its role in the instructional program. For many educators this will require major shifts in attitudes, in resource allocations, and in scheduling; but the result will be students who are far more successful both academically and in the workforce.

## ADDITIONAL RESOURCES

In addition to the resources cited above, you can learn more by accessing these online resources:

American Association of School Librarians: http://www.ala.org/ala/ aasl/aaslindex.htm. This professional organization, which is a division of the American Library Association, advocates for recognition of the importance of school LMCs.

"Strong Libraries Improve Student Achievement" at Education World: http://www.educationworld.com/a_admin/admin/admin178.shtml (2000/2005). This article discusses the role of the school administrator in supporting an effective school library program.

Library Research Service, School Library Impact Studies: http://www .lrs.org/impact.asp. Links to studies, articles, and presentations about the impact of school libraries on student performance.

"Collaboration on the K–5 Level" at the Maine Association of School Libraries Web site: http://www.maslibraries.org/infolit/k5collabstrat .html (n.d.). Concrete strategies for beginning or strengthening teacher/ librarian collaboration.

"Collaboration: Where Does It Begin?" in *Teacher Librarian*, Vol. 9, No. 5, available online at http://www.teacherlibrarian.com/tlmag/v_29/ v_29_5_feature.html (June 2002). An informative article about how teachers and librarians can work together to strengthen instruction.

## QUESTIONS FOR DISCUSSION

1. Does your LMC program incorporate any of the practices described above? Explain.

2. Explain your beliefs about the role an LMC should play on campus.

3. Describe how teachers and librarians at your site/district implement collaboration.

4. What are the benefits and drawbacks of flexible scheduling for LMCs?

5. How is technology used in your school/district LMC? Give examples.

6. What impact does your current site/district LMC program have on student performance? Explain.

# PART II

# *Engaging Teachers and Students*

The first two chapters in this section discuss ways administrators can engage teachers in meaningful professional development that will increase the likelihood that participants will change their practice. The remaining chapters address technology tools and instructional strategies that administrators may encourage teachers to explore and use, remembering that student engagement and increased learning are the ultimate goals.

# 6

---

# *Implementing Your Vision*

## *Professional Development Through Promoting Effective Technology Integration*

> Yogi Berra once said, "You got to be careful if you don't know where you're going, because you might not get there." This is especially true when educators are expected to implement a program without the skills and knowledge required for successful implementation. Rapid changes and capabilities in new technologies make it particularly challenging for teachers and administrators to incorporate their use into professional practice because, in addition to learning new skills, adults must also be open to learning how to do familiar work in new ways.

The school's infrastructure is finally up to par, and the teaching staff includes classroom veterans who have basic technology skills and access to a wealth of on- and off-line electronic resources. An increasing number of students have access to computers and the Internet away from

---

SOURCE: *Today's Catholic Teacher*, October 2002

school. Is it now safe to assume that technology use will impact student learning? According to research, the answer is, "Probably not."

How can this be? For years, educators assumed that lack of equipment and a need for basic training were two of the major impediments to using technology to improve instructional practice; and that once these issues were dealt with, there would be a powerful, and almost immediate, shift in classroom instruction. And yet, this is not happening on a broad scale. Even though most classrooms now have at least one computer and most schools offer access to the Internet as well as a variety of other potentially useful technologies, the actual instruction that's taking place is still business as usual. Technology is most often used to automate traditional assignments rather than to encourage students to approach learning in a new or different way. While there's nothing inherently wrong with using technology to accomplish tasks more easily or quickly, this kind of use has little or no impact on long-term student learning because the basic instructional system hasn't changed. And recent research indicates that this will continue to be the case until educators are able to articulate and implement the next step.

For example, in June 2002, Drs. Douglas W. Green and Thomas O'Brien of Binghamton University published the results of a study conducted in five fifth-grade classrooms at two schools in a district in upstate New York (www.thejournal.com/magazine/vault/A4081.cfm). The teachers participating in the study were seasoned educators and had used technology for several years. Both schools had Internet access and technical support, and teachers had access to professional development opportunities. The study asked two questions:

1. Does Internet use result in increased constructivist teaching practice?

2. Does use of the Internet as an information source for student research projects impact other aspects of classroom practice?

Rather than debate the merits of constructivist teaching practice, let's look at the second question. Drs. Green and O'Brien found that while Internet use appeared to create an environment where students were taking charge of their own learning, in reality the projects were now automated fact-finding exercises. Delving further, Green and O'Brien came to understand that although teachers in the study had opportunities to attend training, most of this professional development consisted of classes on the basics of software operation. Teachers were left to figure out for themselves how software could be used as an instructional tool. As a result, most teachers used the technology to automate existing lessons, rather than as a catalyst to change the fundamental design of the lessons.

This connection between teacher training and classroom implementation also appears in earlier reports, including the West Virginia study released by the Milken Exchange on Education Technology in 1998 (www.mff.org/edtech/article.taf?_function=detail&Content_uid1=127), and the *Technology Counts 98* report published as a joint project by *Education Week* and the Milken Exchange (http://counts.edweek.org/sreports/tc98/). Each report states that basic operational training and access to technology are not enough to ensure changes in teaching styles.

So what does this mean for *your* school? Before you can reasonably expect your technology investment to pay off in ways that extend beyond task automation, the staff needs to work together to accomplish three things:

- Establish a clear vision of the goals of the school's instructional program, and specifically how technology can be used to achieve them.
- Develop an accurate profile of how technology is currently used in classrooms.
- Work cooperatively to develop an ongoing professional development program that is based on curriculum and instruction but includes appropriate technology use along with models of what that use looks like in a classroom.

There is an important caveat here. Teachers cannot be expected to "figure out" technology integration on their own. A realistic assessment of where your school is in technology use and creation of a useful professional development plan must be based upon research on *how teachers learn to become more effective instructional technology users.*

A number of resources can be used as you work through these tasks.

## HOW TEACHERS LEARN TO USE TECHNOLOGY

Studies conducted in the mid- and late 1990s show that individual teachers progress through different levels of use as they learn a new technology and that, to reach more sophisticated levels, ongoing training and support must be offered. One study that clearly explains this progression came out of the Apple Classrooms of Tomorrow (ACOT) project (www.apple.com/education/k12/leadership/acot/).

This study identifies five distinct levels of use teachers experience as they move to successful technology integration:

- **Entry**—Learn the basics of using the new technology.
- **Adoption**—Use the new technology to support traditional instruction. Focus is often on personal use (e.g., making a worksheet) or teaching basic technology skills to students (e.g., keyboarding).
- **Adaptation**—Integrate the new technology into traditional classroom practice. Here teachers often focus on increased student productivity and engagement by using word processors, spreadsheets, and graphics tools.

- **Appropriation**—Shift focus to cooperative, project-based, and interdisciplinary work—incorporating the technology as needed and as one of many tools.
- **Invention**—Discover new uses for technology tools; for example, developing spreadsheet macros for teaching algebra or designing projects that combine multiple technologies.

It's important to understand that even the most experienced users progress through these levels each time they learn to work with a new technology.

In the first three levels, teachers progress from initial exposure to a technology through bringing the technology into the classroom to automate existing activities. However, technology does not become an integral part of instruction until teachers move into levels four and five. Existing professional development programs tend to support the first three levels of use very well, but then drop the ball with the last two levels. This is a primary reason why teachers get stuck in their use of technology with students. Once you can identify various levels of use, you can better measure the current level and quality of technology use in your school and devise a plan to expand that use.

## MEASURING THE QUANTITY AND QUALITY OF TECHNOLOGY INTEGRATION

Determining the current condition of technology integration at your school requires gathering data about both individual teacher proficiency and instructional programs. Self-assessments are not always accurate, but a compilation of results provides an overall profile of strength and weakness. Teachers can use self-assessments to rate personal proficiency and generate individual and group profiles. Two examples of self-assessments are

- **TAGLIT (Taking a Good Look at Instructional Technology):** www .taglit.org
- **Learning With Technology Profile Tool:** www.ncrtec.org/capacity/ profile/profile.htm

The assessments vary in length and emphasis. As a staff, review these and other tools available on the Web, and agree on one that meets your school's needs.

Gathering data about instructional programs is as important as gathering information about personal technology proficiency, because it helps determine how well teachers apply their technology skills in instruction. Educators are often highly skilled technology users, but do not know how to integrate technology use into instruction beyond teaching students how to operate equipment and software. There are existing tools designed specifically to measure this. These include

- **STaR Chart (School Technology and Readiness Chart):** www.iste
  .org/inhouse/starchart/
- **Technology Integration Process Gauge:** www.seirtec.org/eval.html

It is also helpful to use a tool designed to evaluate instructional programs in general. A good example of this type of instrument is Jim Cox's Analysis of Process template available at www.portical.org/d3mtools.html (click on Identify Program Elements to Improve Student Achievement).

After gathering the data, the staff should meet to examine what is reported and observed. What is really happening with technology integration? SouthEast Initiatives Regional Technology in Education Consortium or SEIR♦TEC, the creator of Technology Integration Process Gauge mentioned above, also offers a *Review of the Professional Literature on the Integration of Technology Into Educational Programs* at www.seirtec.org/publications.html. This document can help in your analysis of technology integration.

## Designing a Professional Development Plan

Use the findings from the technology integration review to assist in designing a professional development plan that is curriculum-based and supports teachers in achieving the fourth and fifth levels of technology integration described in the ACOT report. A large body of research on adult learning and professional development, including reports and articles on teachers and technology use, can assist in designing this plan. This research includes

- "Integrating Technology into the Classroom: Eight Keys to Success," *Journal of Teacher Education,* Vol. 10, No. 1, available online at www .aace.org/dl/files/JTATE/JTATE10195.pdf (2002).
- "How Teachers Learn Technology Best," *From Now On; The Educational Technology Journal,* Vol. 10, No. 6: www.fno.org/mar01/ howlearn.html (March 2001).
- "Great Expectations: Beyond One-Shot Workshops," *Northwest Education Magazine,* Vol. 5, No. 4, available online at www.nwrel .org/nwedu/summer00/great.html (summer 2000).

One-time workshops that limit focus to personal productivity may be part of the plan, but are not enough. Teachers need experience in designing and implementing lessons that focus on the curriculum and incorporate technology use that goes beyond automation. Consider these approaches:

- **Individualized professional development plans** One-size-fits-all training models don't work with technology integration. In addition to wide-ranging levels of teaching experience and assignments, you also have the variety of levels of technology experience. By writing comprehensive personal plans, teachers can expand their current skill levels in curriculum, instruction, and technology use.

- **Study groups** By creating self-selected study groups, teachers can identify common areas of concern in curriculum and explore solutions that include use of instructional technology.
- **On-site mentoring** Explore ways to trade some off-site training for on-site coaching. Perhaps someone on staff has the expertise and would be willing to take a modified assignment that includes coaching, or you may be able to work with a consultant who would tailor a coaching program for your site.

# CONCLUSION

Technology use can impact student performance when teachers are prepared to design activities that challenge students to think creatively and solve problems. Teachers can do this with appropriate professional development and support, but they must understand what effective integration looks like before they can hope to accomplish it. It's time to get started!

# ADDITIONAL RESOURCES

In addition to the resources cited above, you can learn more by accessing these online resources:

"Encouraging Teacher Technology Use" at Education World: http://www.education-world.com/a_tech/tech159.shtml (February 2003). A look at how schools encourage (or discourage) teacher use of technology.

National Educational Technology Standards: http://cnets.iste.org/. This project features national technology use standards for students, teachers, and administrators. Visit the NETS for Teachers area to read the standards and performance indicators for teachers.

"Critical Issue: Providing Professional Development for Effective Technology Use" at North Central Regional Education Laboratory: http://www.ncrel.org/sdrs/areas/issues/methods/technlgy/te1000.htm (2000). An in-depth look at professional development to support effective use of technology in classrooms.

"Teachers and Technology: Making the Connection" at Office of Technology Assessment Archive: http://www.wws.princeton.edu/ota/ns20/alpha_f.html (1995). This report explores many aspects of teacher use of technology.

"Just Use It: Rethinking Technology Training for K–12 Teachers": at techLEARNING, http://www.techlearning.com/shared/printable Article.jhtml?articleID=165700672 (August 2005). This article describes a training model where teachers work in collaborative groups to create a curriculum-based project using technology, when appropriate.

## QUESTIONS FOR DISCUSSION

1. List the five ACOT levels of technology use and briefly define each level.

2. In your opinion, what is the most important distinction between levels 1–3 and levels 4–5?

3. Think about current classroom use of technology at your site/district. Where on the continuum of the ACOT levels of use does this use typically fall? Explain.

4. Describe the process you currently use to evaluate teacher use of technology in instruction.

5. How is this information used to increase or improve use of instructional technology? Explain.

6. Does the current professional development program offered in your district support teachers in learning how to use technology beyond level 3 of ACOT? Explain.

7. In your opinion, what professional development approaches are most effective in helping teachers use technology to increase student achievement?

# 7

# *Provide Your Own Professional Development*

Students aren't the only members of the school community who need to be lifelong learners. Educators must also meet this expectation themselves. Fortunately, lifelong learning takes many forms. In addition to traditional methods such as college courses or training seminars, it's now possible to take advantage of a variety of learning experiences offered on- and off-line. Read on to find out more about new and expanded professional development opportunities for educators.

Staying current on new technologies and their classroom applications requires access to information, training, and opportunities to practice what's been learned. Schools may be able to offer teachers a limited amount of professional development, but likely not enough to give most teachers the confidence needed to integrate technology use into classroom practice effectively. How does a teacher fill in the gaps? Thanks to opportunities offered on- and off-line, educators can improve their use of technology

SOURCE: *Today's Catholic Teacher,* March 2005

by engaging in technology-related activities outside of formal training programs. Of course, it's best to couple these activities with a well-designed, ongoing professional development program, but teachers who don't have access to that kind of training can still improve their professional practice.

A number of low-cost and no-cost technology-related activities can supplement the training the school can provide. Most are available online, providing flexibility in timing and pacing. This chapter focuses on four types of activities that can enhance professional growth: conferences and conventions, online courses, Webinars, and professional reading. Explore these resources and take control of your own professional growth.

## CONFERENCES AND CONVENTIONS

Conference attendance alone will not have much impact on classroom practice and should not be the only opportunity taken for professional growth. However, conferences are excellent for learning about trends in educational technology and for developing a network of colleagues for ongoing support and assistance. At one time, teachers interested in learning more about technology use had to attend conferences that specifically targeted this topic. Today many different education-related conferences include technology strands.

If you want to immerse yourself in what's new and what's working in instructional technology, consider attending the National Educational Computing Conference (NECC), sponsored by the International Society for Technology in Education (ISTE). NECC is held each summer and draws attendees from around the world. The program offers hundreds of concurrent sessions, poster sessions, special interest meetings, keynote speakers, and extensive exhibits. ISTE archives a number of sessions online for approximately six months following the conference. For more information on the conference, visit http://www.iste.org/. Many of ISTE's state and regional affiliates also offer their own local technology conferences each year.

If you can't travel to a conference, consider the Imperial Valley Technology Conference, a free virtual conference. First offered in February 2004, and attended by more than 900 educators from 12 countries, the virtual conference offers all the elements of a traditional conference: keynote addresses, sessions and workshops, opportunities to discuss sessions and network with other participants, even a virtual exhibit hall and giveaways! The online venue enables you to attend every session you want when it's convenient for you. Sessions from past conferences are archived and available for viewing at http://library.learningtech.net/. Free registration for the current conference opens in late January. Learn more by visiting the conference Web site at http://conference.learningtech.net.

# ONLINE COURSES

Online courses and workshops come in a variety of formats. Free workshops are self-paced, but do not offer the interactive features of paid courses such as discussion boards and instructor feedback. Paid courses offer an element of self-pacing, but have definite starting and ending dates and sometimes require class members to meet online at a designated time for group chats or other activities. You might want to try a few free offerings before signing up for a fee-based course.

**The National Teacher Training Institute:** www.thirteen.org/edonline/ ntti/resources/index.html. The National Teacher Training Institute (in conjunction with the Educational Broadcasting Corporation's Thirteen/Ed Online), hosts a Web site that offers a wealth of material on using technology in the classroom. The Resources area of this site includes information about using video and the Internet in the classroom, sample lesson plans, and more than a dozen free online workshops. Topics for the workshops range from classroom management strategies to classroom use of the Internet and WebQuests (see Chapter 9).

**Teacher to Teacher Workshops:** www.paec.org/teacher2teacher. The U.S. Department of Education is offering free online courses to all teachers. The workshops are presented by exemplary teachers who share research-based strategies they have used successfully to meet requirements of No Child Left Behind. While many of the workshops are content-based, teachers can also learn a great deal about the strengths and challenges of distance learning by participating in one or more of these courses. Another feature of these workshops is the ability to create an online portfolio which can be accessed during and after the course.

**Teacher Tap:** www.eduscapes.com/tap/. Created by Annette Lamb, this Web site includes online workshops and additional Internet resources for educators. Topics for these free workshops include Overview of Technology-Rich Learning, Technology and Multiple Intelligences, and Evidence-Based Practice and Educational Technology. Fourteen workshops are available currently.

**edutopia:** www.glef.org. The George Lucas Foundation Web site hosts seven free modules for teachers. Each module includes articles, video, PowerPoint presentations, and classroom activities. Module titles include Technology Integration, Project-Based Learning, and Exploratory Learning with a Digital Microscope. This site also offers multimedia presentations of success stories in schools across the nation, video documentaries, and an online magazine.

**PBS TeacherLine:** http://teacherline.pbs.org/teacherline/. PBS TeacherLine has worked with professional educational organizations to develop more than 90 online courses for educators. Many address content areas, but there is also an instructional technology strand. Courses usually run for six weeks and the registration fee is $150. All courses require participants to build digital portfolios and some offer the option of earning graduate credits.

## WEBINARS

Webinars are one-time, live-participation online events. These may be free or fee-based. Typically, organizations that host Webinars archive the events so they can be accessed for free after the fact. The only drawback to relying on the archives is that interactive features are not available.

**techLEARNING T&L Events: Tech Forum and Webinars:** www .techlearning.com/events. techLEARNING offers sponsored Webinars from time to time. Registration is free. You can access the archives of previous Webinars by using the URL provided above and sign up for e-mail notifications of future events. Recent Webinars have addressed such topics as learning communities, mobile computing, and computing access.

**WestEd Regional Technology in Education Consortium:** http://rtecex change.edgateway.net/cs/rtecp/view/rtec_str/3. The WestEd consortium offers occasional online events for teachers. Registration is free, but interactive capabilities are limited to the first 25 registrants. Two event archives and supporting documentation for several past events are currently available. You might also want to look at archives included in the Leadership & Administration tab. Many of these sessions are appropriate for teacher-leaders as well as administrators.

## PROFESSIONAL READING

An excellent strategy for staying on top of new technologies and effective classroom strategies is to skim articles related to these topics on a regular basis. Many publications now make their feature articles available online for quick, free access.

**eSchool News:** www.eschoolnews.com. eSchool News online features include top stories, funding news, and free online newsletters. You can bookmark and visit the site regularly or sign up for one or more free e-newsletters that bring updates directly to your e-mailbox. Free registration is required.

**From Now On:** www.fno.org. This free online journal, published by Jamie McKenzie, is issued 10 times a year. You may subscribe to receive each issue via e-mail or bookmark and visit the site regularly. Article topics include assessment, curriculum, research and information problem-solving, and more. Back issues are archived and available online. This journal invites teachers not only to use technology, but to really think through what they are doing and why.

**4 Teachers.org:** www.4teachers.org. Sponsored by the High Plains Regional Technology in Education Consortium, 4Teachers.org offers links to articles and Web sites addressing a wide variety of topics related to technology use in schools. Presented in two categories, Integrating Technology and Professional Development, each link takes you to an extensive annotated list of Web sites selected for their usefulness for teachers.

Today's students must be prepared to become lifelong learners. One of the most effective ways we can model this behavior for our students is to be lifelong learners ourselves. The Internet, coupled with face-to-face learning opportunities, puts this goal within our grasp.

## ADDITIONAL RESOURCES

In addition to the resources cited above, you can learn more by accessing these online resources:

Association for Supervision and Curriculum Development, Create a Professional Development Plan: http://webserver3.ascd.org/ossd/your_school.html. This template was designed to develop a school professional development plan, but can easily be adapted to develop an individual plan.

"Critical Issue: Providing Professional Development for Effective Technology Use," at North Central Regional Education Laboratory: http://www.ncrel.org/sdrs/areas/issues/methods/tcchnlgy/te1000.htm (2000). This critical issue explores how to plan and incorporate effective professional development for teachers who want to make better use of technology tools in the classroom.

MarcoPolo, Internet Content for the Classroom: http://www.marcopolo-education.org/home.aspx. Well known for high quality online resources and materials, MarcoPolo also offers both online and face-to-face training. One-hour online overview sessions are free. All others are fee-based.

Learner.org, Professional Development Workshops & Courses: http://www.learner.org/. Annenberg offers free multimedia training materials to educators which can be accessed via satellite or online. Videocassettes are also available for purchase. Courses cover a variety of content areas.

Tapped In: http://tappedin.org/tappedin/. Educators may use this site to work collaboratively. Organizations may also develop and implement online classes and webinars through Tapped In.

## QUESTIONS FOR DISCUSSION

1. When is it appropriate to incorporate learning about technology use in professional development? Explain.

2. Describe professional growth activities you have engaged in that included instruction in technology use.

3. When professional growth activities do include instruction in technology use, what kinds of activities are most meaningful for you?

4. When is it appropriate for educators to participate in online professional growth activities?

5. In your opinion, what are the benefits and drawbacks of traditional professional development activities? Explain.

6. In your opinion, what are the benefits and drawbacks of the alternative activities described in this chapter? Explain.

7. What are your personal goals for helping staff access appropriate professional development activities?

# 8

# *Establishing a Web Presence*

## *What to Do Before Building a Classroom Web Site*

In a recent Pew Internet & American Life project survey, more than 80 percent of the teen and parent participants reported they believe that using the Internet has a positive impact on academic performance. There is also a growing public expectation that teachers will have a visible online presence, usually through a school or classroom Web site. Educators who make thoughtful, appropriate use of a Web site stand to gain many benefits; however, building and maintaining a site takes time and perseverance. Teachers and administrators need to take a realistic look at what purpose will be served by a site, and how they plan to make that happen.

Your school's Web site is a big hit with parents. Now the technology team is suggesting that it would be nice for individual teachers to develop their own class Web pages. Or perhaps you've decided on your

SOURCE: *Today's Catholic Teacher,* October 2004

own that you want to design a classroom site. Many schools and individual teachers are exploring the use of teacher-created Web sites either in conjunction with the school's site or as an independent endeavor. But before plunging into becoming a webmaster, you would be wise to lay some groundwork.

Large numbers of schools jumped onto the Web site bandwagon a few years back without giving much thought to why they needed a site or how it would be managed and maintained. The same is true for individual classroom sites. The shoulders of the information highway are littered with teacher pages that say, "Welcome to my classroom," and not a whole lot more. It's common to find sites that offer hopelessly outdated information, suffer from severe cases of link rot (links that do not work), or display "Under Construction" messages in virtually every area. The reasons behind these neglected pages range from "I really didn't want to do this, but was told it was required," to "It was more work than I ever imagined, and I can't keep it up."

On the other hand, there are classroom sites that students and parents visit regularly because they know the sites are well maintained and provide important information they need. While raw enthusiasm is certainly a factor in the success of these sites, there is more to it. Teachers who stick with building and maintaining Web sites that are successful over time usually do so because the benefits their sites offer them, their students, and parents outweigh the work involved. Typically these sites fulfill a clear purpose for a specific audience, and the teachers use design strategies that do not require more time than they are willing or able to spend.

This success can be replicated, but several key areas must be considered first. These include identifying the purpose and benefits of the Web site, understanding school policies and legal issues, and deciding on a workable design format. Throughout this planning process, teachers can visit the Internet to review other teacher-designed Web sites for ideas about what does and does not work and to access free and low-cost tools created to assist in site design. More information about some of these sites is provided later in this chapter.

## DEFINE YOUR SITE'S PURPOSE

A Web site that serves no clear purpose is a waste of time for the developer and for end users. Zero in on the purpose by considering who regular site users will be and what benefits they will derive from visiting the site. Don't attempt to be all things to all possible visitors; it's better to have a fairly narrow focus initially. Students and parents are probably the first logical target groups. It's always possible to add features later for fellow teachers, community members, or other groups.

Once the target audience is established, begin to identify the kinds of information users might want and need. Conduct an informal student survey and a more formal parent survey to ask about their level of interest in a classroom site and the kinds of resources they would like to access and why. Teachers can also draw upon their own experience concerning the types of information and resources parents and children regularly request, and then consider how a Web site might help manage these documents and resources. Using the information collected, make a list of the most frequently requested items.

The next step is to identify the specific benefits a classroom Web site would offer. These might include increased home/school communication, ready access to assignments and resources, or a forum to showcase student work. For example, links to hotlists of Internet sites used in a lesson save students time during class and provide ongoing access to these sites for follow-up work at school or at home. Posting activities updates and examples of student work enables working parents to "visit" the class outside of school hours. Links to homework tips and activities for parents to do at home with their children can be used to extend the school day. But remember, each link or resource included on the site should have a specific benefit associated with it; if this is not the case, it should not be there. In some cases, it may be necessary to refer back to survey responses concerning why parents and students suggested various resources.

Once the benefit for each item on the list is identified, review the list for patterns, and group items into categories such as homework assignments, class news, student work, or online resources for class. If there are too many categories or if the lists of items for each category are lengthy, it may be necessary to prioritize the items in order of importance and plan to address the highest priorities first. It's better to start small and expand the site offerings than to take on too much initially.

## POLICIES AND LEGAL ISSUES

Every school should have an acceptable use policy and a copyright policy in place. There may also be specific policies regarding teacher-created Web sites. Review these documents to learn about existing requirements regarding classroom Web sites. Guidelines might include the kinds of information that may be posted, permissions needed to post student work or photos, rules for linking to outside Web sites, use of graphics, student access to e-mail or discussion boards, or information about linking to the school's official Web site. There may also be restrictions on site design and on who may host the site, such as requiring the use of specific design templates or the school's internet service provider (ISP). If teachers are permitted to choose their own hosting service, they may also be required to pay any subscription fees that are incurred.

Schools that accept E-Rate or other federal funds also must comply with the provisions of the Children's Internet Protection Act (CIPA). These requirements should be reflected in the school's existing policies, but check to be sure. For instance, these requirements would forbid the posting of information, such as last names, that could make a student readily identifiable to an outsider. The site should also be accessible to visitors with disabilities. Once a prototype is designed, each page can be scanned for potential access problems using a tool called Watchfire® Bobby™ 5.0. It's possible to check individual pages using a free online service available at http://webxact.watchfire.com/. Learn more about this tool at http://www.watchfire.com/products/desktop/accessibilitytesting/default.aspx.

## PLAN A USER-FRIENDLY WEB PAGE

Once the preliminary research is completed, it's time to think about the design of the classroom site. Even when page templates are provided, there is usually some latitude given when it comes to setting up links and use of graphics. Reviewing existing classroom Web sites is a great way to get good ideas and to identify pitfalls to be avoided. The sites listed here include links to teacher-designed classroom sites:

- **EduHound Classrooms on the Web:** www.eduhoundclassroomsontheweb.com
- **Cool Classroom Pages:** http://eduscapes.com/tap/topic60.htm
- **MidLink Magazine—Cool Schools:** www.ncsu.edu/midlink/cs/middle.home.html

The primary goals are to create a site that's easy to use and interesting enough to keep parents and students coming back, and that is manageable in terms of the work that must be done to keep it current. Here are some planning tips to help meet these goals.

**Avoiding link overload**—Pages must be easy to read and simple to understand and navigate. Users should not need to scroll to find important links. A frequent mistake made by beginning webmasters is cramming too many links on each page, making it difficult for users to locate the information they need. Instead of showing each individual resource in one place, use the categories developed earlier as titles for links to separate pages where the specific resources can be found. With this approach, the home page itself may have just a few links to areas such as Classroom News, Homework Assignments, Spotlight on Student Work, or Online Activities for Class. This makes it much easier for site visitors to zero in quickly on the type of resource needed, which is then just a click away.

**Careful use of visuals**—Visuals go quickly from being interesting to becoming intrusive. Avoid the temptation to use too many backgrounds, graphics, and animated cursors. In addition to becoming a visual assault that actually interferes with reading the page, maintenance may require more time when each page has its own unique set of graphics. Animated cursors pose a special problem because, unknown to the user, some download unwanted programs in order to show the animation. While such programs are supposed to be harmless, some computers have crashed or had desktop settings altered after one was installed.

**Easy navigation**—When limiting the number of links per page, don't go so far in the other direction that users need to click through multiple pages before finding what they need. A rule of thumb is to limit the number of required clicks to three if possible. An easy way to plan the site is to use a graphic organizer or index cards to lay out a navigation map. Start with the home page and write the links that will be provided there. Then make a card for each of these links. These cards each represent a new page. List the links that will be provided on each new page. Create a new card for each of these links. If these links are subcategories of the main topics, continue this process until you reach the link to the actual document or resource. This approach quickly shows how many clicks will be required to get to a specific resource. It also helps identify where it might be appropriate to add main topic links in a sidebar or tabs across the top of the screen to allow users to jump from one area of the site to another without having to back out the way they came in. Include a Home link on each category and subcategory page.

**Analyzing maintenance requirements**—Once the layout for the site is satisfactory, review the kinds of documents and resources that will be provided. Some of the items will be static, meaning that once they're posted, they can remain unchanged for a long time. This might include classroom rules, a personal introduction, required student supply lists, etc. The remaining items will be dynamic, things that must be updated or changed regularly. The dynamic items will give students and parents a reason to keep returning to the site. They will also determine the amount of time required to maintain the site. It's important to strike a workable balance between the two.

Look at each dynamic item and honestly appraise how often it would need to be changed. Some may be obvious, such as weekly homework assignments. Others may require more thought, such as student artwork. While this should not require weekly updating, the frequency will depend upon what is posted. It's not a good idea for a student showcase still to be featuring autumn leaf rubbings in January! Make a schedule of weekly, monthly, and quarterly updating tasks and decide whether or not it is reasonable. If not, reconsider the frequency of certain updates. Using the artwork example, perhaps a quarterly gallery featuring less time-sensitive work is more realistic. However, to keep parents and students interested, several items must be changed at least monthly.

## NEXT STEPS

With the groundwork laid, it's time to build pages. Check with the school site technology coordinator or webmaster to see what programs or tools are currently in use for building and maintaining the school site and whether they are available to teachers who are building classroom sites. Teachers who must find their own tools and hosting services will find various options on the Internet. There are free hosting sites; however, some may be blocked by school filters, and ads are often included on the site's pages. The two sites listed below offer low-cost site building tools and hosting to educators:

- **TeacherWeb:** http://www.teacherweb.com. A subscription runs $2.50/month or $25/year, when paid in advance.
- **MySchoolOnline:** http://www.myschoolonline.com/golocal. An annual subscription is $39.95.

Teachers, students, and parents reap many benefits from a well-designed classroom page. Take the time upfront to ensure that your classroom's Web presence is the best it can be.

## ADDITIONAL RESOURCES

In addition to the resources cited above, you can learn more by accessing these online resources:

A+ Rubric, Rubric for Classroom Web Pages: http://www.uwstout.edu/soe/profdev/webpagerubric.html. A rubric for evaluating classroom Web pages.

Berrien County Intermediate School District, Web Olympics Scoring Rubric: http://www.remc11.k12.mi.us/rubric.html. A rubric for evaluating school Web sites.

What Makes an Excellent School? http://www.west.asu.edu/achristie/webrubric/. A rubric for evaluating school Web sites.

From Now On, Designing School Web Sites to Deliver: http://www.fno.org/webdesign.html. A collection of articles and resources related to school Web site design.

"The Internet at School" at Pew Internet & American Life Project http://www.pewinternet.org/PPF/r/163/report_display.asp (2005). This recent survey looks at frequency of teen use of the Internet and respondents' opinions about Internet use.

## QUESTIONS FOR DISCUSSION

1. Describe some of the benefits of a classroom Web site.

2. Describe some of the challenges of a classroom Web site.

3. What are the similarities and differences between classroom and school Web sites?

4. What kinds of support should administrators provide to teachers who have (or want to build) a classroom Web site?

5. Using one of the rubrics listed under Additional Resources, visit and evaluate several existing classroom Web sites. (Each site provides a link to a rubric.) What strengths and weaknesses do you find?

6. How could you use the information in your findings for question 5 to provide guidance to teachers in designing their own sites?

7. In your opinion, should teachers be required to design and maintain classroom Web sites? Explain.

# 9

# *Set Out on a WebQuest*

It's a difficult sell to convince students—who regularly use a variety of technologies outside the classroom—that it's just too tough to integrate use of these same tools throughout the school day. And yet, for a variety of reasons, educators persist in trying to do just that. A common explanation is the lack of good instructional models for teachers willing to take the technology plunge. Read on to learn about a Web-based instructional strategy that is easily accessible to all Internet-connected teachers, engages students in meaningful learning, and has a proven track record in impacting student achievement.

If you've wanted to make creative use of the Internet in student instruction but didn't know where to start, you're not alone. *Education Week's* annual *Technology Counts* report for 2001 indicates that while the ratio of computers to students has increased, educators are now having difficulty finding answers to their many questions regarding how students can use technology effectively in their learning.

Technology integration is still new territory for most teachers, and 82 percent of the teachers surveyed for the report said that they do not have enough training or time to develop the kinds of technology-based lessons they would like to use with their students. Most technology-use

SOURCE: *Today's Catholic Teacher,* November/December 2001.

staff development for teachers continues to focus on entry-level proficiencies: Teachers receive little or no guidance on designing and using technology-based lessons that require students to think about concepts and demonstrate their understanding through creative projects.

Students' responses also indicate that computers and other technologies could be better used in the classroom. According to the 500 students in grades 7–12 who were surveyed for the report, computers are used by teachers to cover basics, but often these activities don't relate to what students are currently studying in class and are not structured to help them work with concepts in new ways. Students who do use application software in school report they are generally directed toward use of word processing to write papers or Internet search engines to conduct online research; but typically students are not asked to use technology tools to work with information beyond tracking it down and writing a paper.

Following are several paths you can take to design more effective Internet-based lessons for students. You'll also find helpful models, resources for tools you can use when writing lessons, and examples of lessons created by other teachers.

## WEBQUESTS

One of the best known Internet instructional strategies is the WebQuest, developed in 1995 by Bernie Dodge, professor of educational technology at San Diego State University and long-time proponent of appropriate classroom technology use. Dodge, along with colleague Tom March, created the WebQuest approach to help teachers support student learning through Internet use.

A WebQuest is an activity based on the inquiry instructional approach where most or all of the information used by students is Internet-based. WebQuests can be developed for any content area and are either short-term, requiring one to three classroom sessions to complete, or long-term, taking from a week to a month to finish. The WebQuest approach encourages students to do more than simply find information; they are also asked to make sense of what they find and demonstrate their understanding of material by creating some online or off-line product.

The WebQuest structure consists of six elements:

1. **Introduction**—an explanation of the purpose of the WebQuest and source of background information

2. **Task**—a description of what is to be accomplished by completing the WebQuest

3. **Information sources**—a listing of resources that may include Internet sites, content area experts who are available to students via

email, scheduled video conferences, print materials, and classroom resources

4. **Process**—the steps students take to complete the activity

5. **Guidance**—answers to frequently asked questions students may have about the process, and/or directions for completing specific elements of steps given in the process

6. **Conclusion**—closure for the activity

Dodge's WebQuest page (http://webquest.sdsu.edu/) and the Filamentality site sponsored by Pacific Bell (http://www.filamentality .com/wired/fil/index.html) offer free tools that will walk you through the WebQuest design process.

## ADDITIONAL MODELS

For teachers who want to expand their use of the Internet but aren't ready to tackle a full-blown WebQuest, Filamentality offers four additional fill-in-the-blanks Internet-based lesson design tools.

**Hotlists**—Use this helpful entry-level format when you want students to conduct guided Internet research. Students who are simply given a topic to research and a suggested search engine often waste a great deal of time deciding which sites to review. A hotlist is an annotated collection of related Internet sites that you identify and then direct students to use for researching a topic. This time-saver for students points them toward sites you have reviewed and selected, ensuring that the information they find is valid and relevant.

**Multimedia scrapbook**—This application is still at an entry level, but slightly more sophisticated in terms of student use. A multimedia scrapbook is a collection of sites that you have reviewed and categorized in a particular way, e.g., maps, images, video or audio clips. Students use the scrapbook to find supporting images and documents to use in online or off-line projects. When building a scrapbook, it is very important to include the copyright statement that is provided in the online sample. This statement reminds students that they must get permission from the owners of the sites they visit before downloading images or text to use in a project.

**Treasure hunt**—This activity directs students to specific sites (10–15 are recommended) to answers questions you pose to them. You must review the sites as you develop the treasure hunt to be certain that the answers appear. An activity of this type is most successful when students are working with a topic that holds high interest for them but about which they have little or no background information. While you can develop simple comprehension-level questions, students will benefit more from working with questions that require them to think creatively. Close the activity with a question that lets students interpret the information they have gathered and explain what they have learned.

**Subject sampler**—Samplers work well for students who already have some background information about a topic and are looking for an interesting approach. The online tool enables you to build a list of Internet sites (six is recommended) that address a related topic. Students are asked to visit each site in the sampler and answer questions you have prepared about the subject. Completing the sampler helps students decide where their interests lie regarding the subject. They can work from there to design and complete a larger project.

## HOW MUCH TIME DOES IT TAKE?

The time required to plan and use Internet-integrated lessons varies depending upon the lesson type and whether you develop your own or use existing lessons; but it definitely takes more time to begin with. At the very least you must spend time searching for and reviewing existing lessons. Online resources for existing WebQuests and other Internet-based lessons are given below.

Creating your own lesson requires identifying objectives, developing activities, and creating an assessment tool as usual. Then you must search for sites to use in the lesson. Searching takes practice but is facilitated by a good search engine such as Google.com or Yahoo.com. Check sites carefully before recommending them for students. Kathy Schrock offers several Web site evaluation forms at http://school.discovery.com/schrockguide/eval.html. A similar rubric is available from Seabury Hall school at www.seaburyhall.org/library/evaluate1.html.

Once you have researched sites, you're ready to develop your own Internet-based lessons.

## CLASSROOM IMPLEMENTATION

As you select or write an Internet-based lesson, bear in mind what kind of Internet access you have and how you will use the lesson in the classroom. Will all work take place in the classroom or will your class go to a computer lab? Does your school have an Intranet that allows you to store the WebQuest and linked sites on a file server, making an actual Internet connection unnecessary? It is possible to use Internet-based lessons under less-than-ideal conditions, but it requires thought and planning.

Using this type of lesson may change your approach to instruction because these lessons are often written based on the expectation that students will work in small, collaborative groups where they control the pacing of their tasks. Culminating activities generally ask students to use critical thinking skills to apply their new learning. You may assume a support role with students and use less direct instruction.

If your interest is piqued and you want to learn more about these creative uses of the Internet with students, go straight to Bernie Dodge's WebQuest Page at http://webquest.sdsu.edu/. You will find information and a matrix of sample WebQuests. The Filamentality site (http://www.filamentality.com/wired/fil/index.html) also offers Blue Web'n, a library of award winning Internet sites for librarians and teachers. It includes samples of the activities you can develop using the templates at the site. Use the examples as guides to developing your own lessons or have your students work with the existing lessons that support your curriculum.

Kathy Schrock's Guide for Educators site also includes a page devoted to WebQuests. You will find more information about the development of WebQuests along with links to sites that have sample WebQuests at http://school.discovery.com/schrockguide/webquest/webquest.html.

Internet-based activities are exciting and rewarding for students and teachers. The resources available to you through the WebQuest Page and Filamentality will guide you toward successful, innovative Internet experiences for your class.

## ADDITIONAL RESOURCES

In addition to the resources cited above, you can learn more by accessing these online resources:

Best WebQuests: http://bestwebquests.com/. Tom March, cocreator of WebQuests, hosts this site where you can find links to high quality WebQuests.

Dr. Alice Christie's Matrix of 320 WebQuests: http://www.west.asu .edu/achristie/wqmatrix.html. K–12 WebQuests designed by university students.

Locate and Evaluate WebQuests: http://eduscapes.com/tap/topic4 .htm. Annette Lamb created this extensive list of Web links to resources for WebQuests.

Understanding and Using WebQuests: http://midgefrazel.net/ lrnwebq.html. Midge Frazel built this list of resources for a teacher workshop.

WebQuest Portal: http://webquest.org/. Bernie Dodge blogs about WebQuests.

## QUESTIONS FOR DISCUSSION

1. If asked, what would students in your school/district say about how technology is being used to support learning and teaching?

2. Do you think that your students are satisfied with the current level of use of instructional technology in your site/district? Explain your answer.

3. List and describe the six elements of a WebQuest.

4. How does a WebQuest differ from using the Internet for basic research?

5. Visit the Filamentality site and click on A Tour of the Process. Which of the Filamentality tools appeal most to you? Explain your answer.

6. In your opinion, which of the Filamentality tools would be most appealing to teachers? Explain your reasoning.

7. Describe how use of this kind of tool could enhance or expand effective use of instructional technology at your site/district.

# 10

# Blogs in K–12 Education

## *Where's the Fit?*

Quick access and ease of use are two critical factors administrators must be able to address when encouraging teachers to increase their use of technology. Many educators are reluctant to incorporate use of the Web in activities, or as a tool for communication, due to the fact that they are dependent upon someone else to get postings updated because they lack the skills (or permission) to do it themselves. The weblog, a relatively new online tool, enables anyone who can enter text into a file to easily design and maintain an online environment. This chapter explores ways to incorporate use of weblogs in schools.

Across New York City, residents used weblogs to write about the events of 9/11 as they happened: what they were doing, what they saw, how they coped. The result is an online collection of eyewitness accounts and photo galleries from that devastating time. A weblog called Where is Raed? written by "Salam Pax" described events in Baghdad before, during, and after the American invasion. His postings about life

SOURCE: *Today's School*, November/December 2004

in Iraq during the fall of Saddam Hussein's regime eventually won worldwide attention. Howard Dean's campaign for the 2004 presidential nomination used a Web site and weblog to raise support and funding, receiving $7.4 million in online contributions during one quarter of 2003.

Press coverage of these and other high-profile weblogs has brought this form of computer-mediated communication (CMC) to the attention of the mainstream. But use of weblogs actually began at least a decade ago when they were created by programmers to post lists of links to recommended Web sites. In fact, the term *weblog* was coined in the late 1990s.

A *weblog*, usually shortened to *blog*, is a Web site that consists of dated entries presented in reverse chronological order so that the most recent posts appear first. Some consider them "online diaries." The development of blog hosting sites over the last few years has made it extremely easy for nonprogrammers to create their own blogs. As a result, the number of bloggers has grown and the content of these blogs varies widely as users explore ways to communicate. Even with experimental approaches, there are three common forms taken by blogs:

**Personal blogs**—usually the work of one author who writes about his or her personal views on a topic. Readers of the blog may post comments about the entries. Personal blogs may be configured to allow more than one person to post original entries. It is also possible to restrict access to the blog, depending upon the features of the blog host or installed application used to create the blog.

**Organizational blogs**—used by some groups to communicate internally (e.g., teacher to teacher, teacher to student) or externally (e.g., principal to parents, teacher to parents) in lieu of more traditional Web sites because they are easier to maintain or update and allow for some interactivity.

**Commercial blogs**—used by businesses as a marketing tool, but the most worthwhile blogs are short on advertising and offer readers useful information, including links to articles and other resources. The National School Board Association's BoardBuzz (http://boardbuzz.nsba.org/) is an example of a blog provided by a professional organization.

## WHO IS BLOGGING?

While its popularity has grown, two recent reports indicate that blogging is still in its infancy. The Pew Internet & American Life Project (www .pewinternet.org/report_display.asp?r=113) conducted a telephone survey of American adults between March 12 and May 20, 2003, and again in early 2004. While 44 percent of the Internet users surveyed in 2003 said they had posted information to the Web, just 2 percent reported creating their own blogs. The follow-up survey indicates that this number has increased to 7 percent, and that 11 percent of the respondents had read a blog authored by someone else. But these statistics are no surprise to those who think of blogging as being the domain of teens and young adults.

Perseus Development Corporation (http://www.perseus.com/blogsurvey/) conducted a random survey of 3,634 blogs on eight popular blog hosting sites to get a handle on who is blogging. The findings are reported in a document titled *The Blogging Iceberg.* As might be expected, teenagers (51.5 percent) and young adults ages 20–29 (39.6 percent) created 91.1 percent of the blogs surveyed. Overall, most of the blogs (56 percent) were created by females. However, there were some surprises. Although Perseus projects that 10 million blogs will be created by the end of 2004, the survey showed that 66 percent of the blogs reviewed had been temporarily or permanently abandoned, meaning they had not been updated in at least two months. Of the blogs that had been abandoned, 40 percent had entries for just one day, and the average lifespan of the rest was approximately four months. Another surprise: The average active blog is updated just once every two weeks and is clearly intended for small audiences including family, friends, or fellow students. Conclusions drawn in the report state that, despite the few high-profile blogs that are frequently updated and draw thousands of readers, typical blogs are actually written by teenaged girls for their friends and classmates and are updated twice each month.

## HOW IS THIS INVOLVED WITH EDUCATION?

It's fair to say that educators who are using blogs themselves or with their students are on the leading edge with this technology. There is keen interest in the potential uses of blogging among technology-using educators. More than 17,000 educators from around the world gathered in New Orleans for the 2004 National Educational Computing Conference, which featured several standing-room-only sessions and workshops on blogging, as well as a popular Weblogging Birds of a Feather meeting.

Although it's still evolving, this communication form is highly appealing to a large segment of our student population and may prove to be a great tool for adults as well. It's to our benefit to examine the strengths of blogging and capitalize on them in schoolwide and classroom communication. It may also be useful to conduct this examination through the lens of the findings of the Apple Classrooms of Tomorrow research (http:// images.apple.com/education/k12/leadership/acot/pdf/10yr.pdf), published in 1995. The report (covered more fully in Chapter 6) describes five stages of use teachers experience when using a new technology: entry, adoption, adaptation, appropriation, and invention. As readers will recall, it's not until stages four and five that teachers are comfortable enough with the new technology to begin exploring uses that might change their instructional style.

Keeping these findings in mind, educators can use information from surveys such as the ones cited earlier to develop activities that support administrators, teachers, and students at early stages of use and still provide meaningful experiences. For example, although the media may hype access to worldwide audiences, the Perseus survey shows that, when left to their own devices, bloggers are actually targeting a much smaller group— usually people they know. This means educators might want to begin by creating and using their own blogs, either individually or in small groups, simply to gain firsthand knowledge about this communication form and to figure out ways to share important information with their peers. This provides an opportunity to learn the basics, experiment with targeting audiences, and try out various security levels. In addition, by blogging themselves, administrators and teachers can determine realistic goals for frequency of new entries, handling comments, and a blog's life expectancy. Once the adults are comfortable with these early levels of use, they can begin using blogs with students.

Of course, achieving the adaptation level in classrooms would be just the beginning. Hopefully, once teachers and students are comfortable with automating traditional assignments, they would begin to explore more creative uses. In the meantime, here are some examples of ways that early users are making use of blogs in schools and classrooms.

## WEBLOG WEB SITES FOR SCHOOLS

A growing number of schools are using blogging software to create a Web presence for their school. Ease of design and maintenance are major factors in this decision, but so is the fact that multiple users are able to update the site without needing to funnel changes through a webmaster. The potential for interaction using RSS (an acronym that refers to several different technologies that inform blog subscribers of updated entries and comments) and the discussion capability of blogs are also viewed as plusses. Of course, the possibility of inappropriate entries increases when more people are able to post. However, it is possible to moderate entries so that they must be approved before they are published. While this impedes the process somewhat, entries awaiting approval may be e-mailed directly to the moderator to make changes or give permission to post. Will Richardson, supervisor of instructional technology at Hunterdon Central Regional High School in Flemington, New Jersey, has blogged about the process his school has used to design and launch a weblog (www.web logg-ed.com).

Most current school blogs look very much like traditional Web sites, except that in some cases, a Discuss link appears at the bottom of entries.

It will be interesting to see how these blogs mature and grow. Here are a few weblogs to visit:

- **Butlerville Elementary School:** www.butlerville.net. A K–4 school in Blanchester, Ohio
- **Meriwether Lewis Elementary School:** http://lewiselementary.org. A K–5 school in Portland, Oregon
- **Delano High School:** www.delanohighschool.org. A high school in Delano, California
- **Hunterdon Central Regional High School:** www.hcrhs.k12.nj.us. A high school in Hunterdon County, New Jersey

## BLOGS IN CLASSROOMS

A growing number of teachers are using blogging software rather than traditional Web sites to establish their classroom sites. Blogs are easier to create and maintain and it's still possible to set up links to various areas, so they have the look and feel of regular Web sites. This is an excellent way to learn the basics and experiment with interactivity in a controlled environment.

Several teachers at Butlerville Elementary School blog their classroom pages. Mrs. Carmack, a first-grade teacher at Butlerville, regularly posts on her Carmack's Critters weblog at www.butlerville.net/1a. She also offers sidebar links where parents and students may access information about show and tell, spelling words, word-wall words, etc.

Julie Ringold and Kris Dinnison teach sophomore humanities at Mead High School in Spokane, Washington, and use a blog (www.mead.k12.wa .us/mhs/hanson/home.htm) rather than a traditional classroom Web site to share the syllabus, resources, readings, and assignments.

One of the frequently suggested entry/adoption-level blogging exercises for students is automated personal journals. Each student creates a personal blog and uses it in lieu of a traditional bound journal. Access levels may be set so that entries are available just to the teacher, to selected friends, or to other classmates so authors can receive comments from their peers as well as the teacher. Teachers and other readers are able to monitor entries using RSS notifications for new entries. While this is a feasible management strategy, it's important for teachers to think the logistics through carefully. Privacy is an issue even with hardcopy journals. When students are asked to post personal entries online, care must be taken to ensure that the entries are only accessible to the student author and teacher unless the student intentionally makes a post public to other classmates. Public postings should be optional, not required.

In addition to journals, teachers are using blogs to ask students to respond to writing prompts or topics of interest such as sports or movies.

This adoption/adaptation strategy automates traditional writing assignments and may increase student productivity, as the approach appeals to many students. In addition to moving toward a paperless classroom, students can bolster their technology skills as they learn to use various capabilities of the blog software to incorporate graphics and audio into their posting along with links and text formatting to enhance their writing. There is also the allure of writing for a wider audience, including fellow students, parents, and other visitors. This type of blogging may be set up for individuals or groups; here are some examples:

- Bob Sprankle's third- and fourth-graders post news and other writing throughout the school year. Visit his Room 208 blog at http://bobsprankle.com/blog/.
- Ann Davis works at Georgia State University in the Instructional Technology Center in the College of Education. She regularly engages in blog projects that involve students and teachers. Her most recent project, A School of Voices (http://itc.blogs.com/) invites K–12 students and teachers to participate in online discussions. Previous projects include Thinking and Writing Wrinkles (http://anvil.gsu.edu/Wrinkles), written by fifth-grade students, and NewsQuest (http://anvil.gsu.edu/NewsQuest/), a blog for upper elementary students learning media awareness and critical thinking skills.
- Elizabeth Fullerton teaches senior English at Columbia Central High School in Columbia, Tennessee. She and her students blog regularly, and Fullerton is pleased by the results. "Blogging seems to teach critical thinking and Internet research skills, as well as enhancing writing skills," she said. The students' writings are available at www.elizabethfullerton.com.
- When Will Richardson taught journalism, his students used blogs to complete assignments throughout the course. An example of one of his students' blogs can be accessed at http://weblogs.hcrhs.k12.nj.us/meredithf. Richardson's literature students read the book *The Secret Life of Bees* by Sue Monk Kidd and use a blog (http://weblogs.hcrhs.k12.nj.us/beesbook) to summarize the chapters, post artistic interpretations, discuss symbolism in the text, and more. When students had questions about the book, Richardson contacted the author. Her responses to the students are accessible through the Schedule link.
- Two fourth-grade teachers in Galloway, New Jersey, paired up with two teachers in Katy, Texas, to have their students also pair up to participate in a collaborative online project as they read *Sarah, Plain and Tall*. Each student posted journal entries on the blog and had the opportunity to respond to his or her partner's entry. The blog is available at http://caxton.stockton.edu/sarahplainandtall.

## BLOGGING AND ADMINISTRATORS

A handful of principals are experimenting with writing blogs to post regular entries to staff or students. During the 2004–05 school year, Joyce Hooper, principal of J. H. House Elementary School in Conyers, Georgia, authored a blog called Principal's Quest (http://itc.blogs.com/principal squest). She posted weekly entries aligned with the school's character education program. The blog was accessible to staff and students to read and make comments.

Two of the weblogs mentioned earlier are maintained by the schools' principals, Pamela Coates at Butlerville Elementary and Tim Lauer at Meriwether Lewis Elementary School. Lauer reports, "We use the weblog/ school site as a place to post items in anticipation of also publishing them in paper form in the weekly letter that is sent home to each family. This allows us to make the information more timely while at the same time making sure we share the same information via paper with our families that may not access the Web."

Teachers' weekly classroom notes posted online are also included in the print newsletter. In addition, Lauer blogs the staff bulletin. "I use this forum for many of the day-to-day announcements that can sometimes consume staff meeting time. By using the staff bulletin weblog, teachers can comment on items there, and we are able to free up more meeting time to work on practice and instruction and looking at student data."

Additional ideas are surfacing for ways for administrators to use blogs for sharing and gathering information. Examples include blogging with grade-level groups of teachers to discuss issues surrounding curriculum and instruction, documenting committee work for review and comment, or blogging memos to staff.

## BLOGGING TOOLS

If all this has piqued your interest, you may want to know where to find resources and tools to help get you started. A number of Web sites offer free or low-cost easy-to-use blog hosting services. These sites are good starting points for educators with little or no programming experience. It's important to check out the terms of service to find out whether the no-cost blogs are free of advertising. Here are several hosting sites frequently used by educators:

- **Blogger:** www.blogger.com. Around since 1999, Blogger is a free service.
- **Blog Meister:** http://epnweb.org/blogmeister/index.php?display= blogmeister. Hosted by the Landmark Project, this free tool is designed specifically for classroom use.

- **TeacherHosting:** www.teacherhosting.com. TeacherHosting offers low-cost blogging options to teachers and other educators. Blog subscription pricing begins at $5/month. Additional features are available at additional cost.
- **TypePad:** www.typepad.com. Subscription pricing ranges from Basic (one blog for $4.95/month) through Pro (an unlimited number of blogs for $14.95/month).

More advanced users may choose to download installed applications to their own Web sites. The benefit of an installed application is that you control access to blogs, an important feature for K–12 schools. Popular installed applications include the following:

- **Manila:** http://manila.userland.com. One-time price is $1,099, but education discounts are available.
- **Movable Type:** www.movabletype.org. This offers a free, unsupported version in which one author may maintain up to three blogs. K–12 packages are offered at one-time prices ranging from $39.95 for a single classroom up to $1,299.95 for up to 3,000 students.
- **WordPress:** http://wordpress.org. This is a free personal publishing platform.

It's exciting to have the opportunity to explore a new communication form and to take part in defining how it will be used in schools. It's also important to remember that first use often ends up becoming entrenched use. As educators experiment with the use of blogs, we must keep open minds and continue to expand our thinking about how this tool can support instruction.

## ADDITIONAL RESOURCES

In addition to the resources cited above, you can learn more by accessing these online resources:

"What's in a Blog?" in *American School Board Journal,* Vol. 192, No. 7, available online at http://www.asbj.com/2005/07/0705coverstory2 .html (July 2005). An overview of blogging for school administrators.

EdBlogger Praxis: http://educational.blogs.com/edbloggerpraxis/. A good place to find examples of educator blogs.

ed-tech insider: http://www.eschoolnews.com/eti/index.php. *eSchool News* hosts this blog which focuses on critical issues in education.

NECC 2004, Blogs and Wikis as WebQuest Tasks: http://webquest
.sdsu.edu/necc2004/blogs-and-wikis.htm. Summary of a presentation
made by Bernie Dodge at NECC 2004.

EduBlog Insights: http://anne.teachesme.com. Pioneer blogger Anne
Davis shares insights and resources related to classroom use of blogs.

## QUESTIONS FOR DISCUSSION

1. Based upon your reading, how could use of blogs benefit
   students and teachers?

2. Based upon your reading, what are some potential pitfalls educators need to keep in mind regarding use of blogs in schools?

3. If you were going to assist in developing a blog use policy, what
   steps would you take and what provisions would you want to
   include?

4. Describe two administrative uses for blogs.

5. If your school/district adopted use of blogs, would you use a
   commercial blog site host, or download and manage blog software in-house? Explain your reasoning.

6. Many educators have resisted use of personal Web sites due to
   the amount of work required to design and maintain a site. How
   could blog software address these concerns?

7. Recent studies show that increasing numbers of middle and
   high school students blog outside of school, raising concerns
   about Internet safety. How would you address these concerns
   with students in your school/district?

# 11

Video Streaming

*Harnessing a Unique Capability of Technology*

> There is growing interest in classroom use of digital video. However, getting started requires more time and effort than many educators anticipate, leading to limited implementation. Why is this instructional strategy worth the extra time, money, and effort? Because increasing numbers of students who have access to a wealth of multimedia technologies away from school are disengaging from classroom instruction. It's not a silver bullet, but effective incorporation of digital video can engage students and support instruction.

U se of audiovisual tools increases student attention and retention of information. But it hasn't always been easy to regularly integrate use of audiovisuals into instruction. Thirty years ago, showing a movie or filmstrip during class required a lot of preparation and change in routine. The teacher needed to find and order an appropriate film (and hope it arrived on time), sign up to use a projector, and sometimes reserve a space that could be darkened enough to actually see the film and still accommodate a class.

SOURCE: *Today's School*, May/June 2005

Due to the physical limitations of threading and running a projector, movies were shown from start to finish—even when a five-minute segment would have been sufficient to meet the teacher's objective.

Fifteen years ago, the availability of fairly inexpensive VCRs and portable televisions made it possible for teachers to increase their use of audiovisuals and to experiment with presentation techniques. Unlike film, it was easy to cue a tape to view a specific sequence or to replay segments for additional review. But use of videotape had its limitations as well. Teachers still needed to select a video and check for its availability. VCRs and televisions were usually shared and had to be reserved. Initial cueing for one segment was easy enough, but when teachers wanted to use multiple short clips, the flow of the lesson was disrupted while they found the next segment or switched tapes. And so, although videotape was a vast improvement over film, its use wasn't transparent.

Advances in video, film, and computer technologies during the 1990s opened the door for new approaches in instructional use of audiovisuals. The ability to convert images from videotape or film into digital format was a major step. Videos and films could be stored on a digital video disc (DVD). They could also be saved on a massive storage device and viewed using a computer. It was possible to skip from one segment of a video to the next by clicking a remote, or to download and show short video clips from the Internet. This increased flexibility in accessing and viewing digitalized video set the stage for teachers who wanted to use video in more meaningful ways.

Today, with the growing numbers of classrooms with Internet-connected multimedia computers, increased availability of DVDs, and access to online collections of educational videos and clips, teachers are positioned to make regular, effective use of digital video in classrooms, and interest is growing. Quality Education Data (www.qeddata.com) reports that 26.7 percent of schools in the United States are now using digital video via video streaming in classrooms, and another 32.1 percent are evaluating its use for adoption in the near future.

The drive to explore this new instructional technique couldn't come at a better time. Many administrators and teachers recognize that traditional approaches to instruction are not meeting the needs of today's students. Children of the digital age come to school with very different experiences and expectations than their predecessors and they are disenchanted with the industrial-age approach to education.

## STUDENTS' SHIFTING PERCEPTIONS

According to the National Center for Education Statistics (NCES), the majority of students who graduate from high school today believe that school is irrelevant. In 1983, 51 percent of seniors surveyed believed that things they learned in school would be important later in life. By 2000, just 39 percent held the same belief. In addition, much smaller percentages of seniors in 2000 believed that their schoolwork was meaningful or that courses were interesting. Students participating in the Northwest Regional Educational Laboratory's (NWREL) School Change Collaborative also report that they do not believe that schoolwork is relevant, stating that their experiences away from school are more meaningful and valuable to them.

What are the kinds of experiences that students value? A study from the Kaiser Family Foundation, released in March 2005 (http://www.kff .org/entmedia/entmedia030905pkg.cfm), reports that an increasing number of children ages 8 to 18 now have multimedia centers in their bedrooms where they can surf the Internet, listen to music, watch television, play video games, and more. Even in homes where technology is placed in public spaces, 39 percent now have two or more computers and 74 percent have Internet access. The children surveyed reported spending an average of six or more hours per day using media at home.

Students participating in the NWREL collaborative think that classroom instruction would be improved if teachers would vary their instructional methods and use more creativity. Suggestions for change include fewer lectures and less whole-class instruction, and more time for active learning. Digital video can be used to address these suggestions because it lends itself well to various instructional strategies and more active learning using a medium that students know and value.

## HOW ARE TEACHERS ACCESSING DIGITAL VIDEO?

Teachers are using DVDs, online videos and clips, and even creating their own digital videos. Because this chapter focuses on the use of existing digital video, the following discussion targets just the first two sources.

Commercially produced DVDs are readily available. Although teachers may not have a separate DVD player, most new computers have the capability of playing a DVD, so a computer and a means to project an image are all that's required. Because this technology is popular in homes, most teachers have the skills to skip around the disc, accessing individual chapters or scenes in any order. But using a DVD leaves the door open for continued accessibility issues. Unless the teacher owns the DVD, there is still the need to order the disc and then rely on the hope that it will be available when it's needed.

Internet-based videos and clips answer this concern. Using an online library (in most instances), teachers are able to download and use short videos and clips as needed. There is also the option of viewing videos and clips directly from the Internet. This is referred to as streaming video.

## WHAT IS STREAMING VIDEO?

Most computers cannot download complete video files quickly. Streaming is a method for data transfer that allows the user to begin watching a video while data is still being transferred. The data is sent to an application such as QuickTime Player or Windows Media Player, which converts it to pictures or sound. The rate of data transmission is determined by network's bandwidth. The greater the bandwidth, the more data can be transmitted during a fixed period of time. When data is received faster than it can be processed by the application, it is temporarily stored in a buffer and processed as needed. However, when the data stream is too slow, the video is jerky and the sound starts and stops. School networks often have less bandwidth than is optimal for video streaming. Downloading video files onto a server ahead of time can circumvent this. Then, when the file is actually viewed, the speed of the Internet connection or the volume of traffic on the network is not an issue.

## WHAT ARE THE BENEFITS OF AN ONLINE DIGITAL VIDEO LIBRARY?

Video and film collections maintained by schools, districts, and even regional offices are often limited in size and content due to the costs involved in maintaining comprehensive collections. Even when a title appears to be a good fit, unless a teacher is able to go to the place where the collection is housed and arrange to use equipment to preview the video, it's often difficult to determine whether the material covered actually supports a lesson. An alternative is to order the video twice, once for previewing and once for classroom use, but most ordering and delivery systems aren't conducive to double booking. Therefore, unless it is something a teacher has used previously, choosing a video is often a shot in the dark. Using an online digital video library addresses these challenges.

Imagine having access thousands of videos and short clips that have been reviewed for alignment to content and curriculum standards. Using a searchable database, it is possible to browse the collection by content or standard area or to generate a list of videos and clips that are the best matches. Once the possibilities have been identified, teachers can view the actual videos or clips immediately or at a more convenient time, then make selections, knowing that there will be no problems with availability. Depending upon the type of subscription purchased, it is possible to request that the video be downloaded for classroom use, or to simply retrieve it from the Internet or a local server when needed. It is also possible to review and download supporting teaching guides and lesson plans. In theory, this work can even be done at home. Teachers who have high-speed Internet access at home will be able to access and use the online collection with little or no difficulty. However, teachers who still rely on a dial-up connection may encounter problems.

## WHAT ARE THE DRAWBACKS?

As is the case with any relatively new technology, teachers will find that digital libraries do have some drawbacks. Having access to thousands of titles and clips is an exciting prospect. However, it takes time to become familiar with all the resources. When first implementing use of a digital library, teachers may find that selecting the videos they want to use requires more time than they'd imagined. The quality of the content and presentation will vary, so it's important to take a close look at each clip. Taking full advantage of this medium also requires that teachers rethink lesson plan design. While just watching a clip may perk up student interest, critical viewing will lead to greater understanding. This means that the teacher must plan how to introduce the video, what will occur while students watch the video, and meaningful follow-up activities.

When a school invests in a subscription to an online video library, it's also wise to set aside funds for professional development. Teachers will make better use of the collection when they have received instruction on how to find and access materials. It is also important to ensure that teachers understand how to design lessons that effectively incorporate use of digital video.

Bandwidth may be a stumbling block. Before purchasing a subscription, administrators and teachers should work closely with technical staff to identify what they want to do and whether or not the existing network can handle the proposed traffic. If network upgrades are recommended, take care of these before attempting to implement use of the online library. Vendors recognize that this is an issue for schools and offer various options to help get around the problems. Invite vendors to come to the site and demonstrate how these options would work in the existing environment.

## TIPS FOR USING DIGITAL VIDEO CLIPS

Using brief clips is very different from devoting an entire period to watching a video. Maximizing the impact of the clip(s) requires careful preplanning and adjustments in instructional strategies. While they don't take the place of well-designed professional development, here are 10 tips for making effective use of clips:

- **Keep it short.** In most cases, three to five minutes is more than enough time to get the point across. If the clip is longer than that, view it again critically. Is it really necessary to show the entire clip, or is it possible to get to the heart of the matter in less time? If it seems important to show the entire clip, consider segmenting it. Show part of the clip. Stop for discussion or an activity, and then show the rest.

- **Choose a variety of clips.** Depending upon their content, clips may be used for many purposes, such as introducing a topic, illustrating a concept, or setting up a learning scenario. Unfortunately, first use tends to become the entrenched use, and teachers often get stuck using clips for just one purpose. Keep lessons lively and interesting by intentionally varying the reason for using a clip.

- **Listen to the clip's soundtrack carefully.** Some clips are more effective or can be used across a broader range of grade levels when the sound is turned off. Consider showing the video accompanied by teacher commentary rather than always relying on the soundtrack.

- **Avoid using "talking head" clips.** Students won't retain more information from a lecture simply because it's digitized.

- **Use a wireless presentation remote to start and stop clips.** This allows the teacher to move around the classroom and still control the presentation.

- **Keep downloaded clips and links organized.** It will be easy to find files. However, if files are kept on a computer for later use, teachers will lose track of them in no time. Bookmark the clips or links needed for a lesson, or import them into a PowerPoint file. This allows for easy transitions from one clip to the next without searching the desktop or folders to find a missing file.

- **Ask the following questions before using a clip:** How does use of the clip meet the lesson objectives? What will students gain by watching it? What will students to do with the information provided? Would there be a better way to present this information?

- **Do not allow students to be passive viewers.** Set the stage by giving a brief overview and having focus questions for students to think about while they're watching. When appropriate, ask students to make predictions about what they think will happen during the clip and then watch to see if their predictions are accurate.

- **On occasion, it may be appropriate to ask students to view one or more clips before a lesson.** Try this technique as an anticipatory set to set the stage for a lesson.

- **When planning a lesson, include time for clips to be reviewed more than once.** This is especially important when students are asked to engage in activities directly related to the clip(s).

Don't confine use of an online library to staff. Think about ways students can use these resources to demonstrate learning. Encouraging this kind of activity will promote student engagement and increase retention of material, particularly if students are asked to present their projects to the class or other audience.

Teachers and administrators must also familiarize themselves with the copyright agreement that governs use of the digital video library. There may be provisions about how long teachers are allowed to store clips. In most instances it is legal for students to use the digital library to find and use clips in their own projects, but there may still be limitations. For example, look to see if student projects may be posted on a classroom or school Web page.

## WHERE TO LEARN MORE ABOUT ONLINE DIGITAL VIDEO LIBRARIES

Several state departments of education, such as those of Arkansas, Nebraska, and Rhode Island, now offer their districts free access to online digital video libraries. Before talking with vendors, check to see it your state has this kind of program. If you need to strike out on your own, two popular options are BrainPOP and unitedstreaming.

**BrainPOP:** www.brainpop.com. This site is especially attractive to elementary and middle schools. This subscription-based Web site includes several hundred standards-aligned offerings for math, science, health, English, social studies, and technology. The two- to five-minute animated movies are organized by content and skill areas in searchable libraries. Each movie has an accompanying 10-question interactive quiz, comic strip, experiment, timeline, printable activity, and links to related movies. The teacher section provides further support in the form of lesson plans, ideas for use, and standards correlations. This site is especially useful for teachers who are just beginning to use digital video. While the choices are plentiful, they're not overwhelming, and the supporting materials for every movie are helpful. Pricing ranges from $134.95 for a one-year teacher subscription to $1.44/student for districts of 1,000+ students. Students have free access from home to two BrainPOP movies each day. To learn more about BrainPOP, visit the Web site and review the presentation movie, an animated introduction to the site.

**unitedstreaming:** www.unitedstreaming.com. This site, owned by Discovery Communications, currently provides a collection of more than 4,000 full educational videos and 40,000 content clips that may be searched by keyword, subject, topic, grade level, or academic standard. To help customize use, subscribers are able to select from full videos, shorter video chapters, or brief video segments. The site also includes an image library, clip-art gallery, quiz center, lesson plans, teacher's guides, and more. Schools have three subscription options: Internet, local host, or network manager. The first option allows schools to stream and download video directly from the Internet. This subscription does not require a local server, but can be impacted by the speed of the school's Internet connection.

The local host option allows subscribers to download all unitedstreaming content onto a local server. Updates to the unitedstreaming collection are automatically downloaded to the subscriber's server. The network manager subscription allows schools to download just those videos, chapters, and segments specifically requested by teachers. Once downloaded, videos may be viewed without impacting bandwidth. Pricing varies. A network manager subscription starts at a base price of $299, and other subscriptions are $1,495/year for high schools or $995/year for elementary schools. Multiyear discounts are available.

With the demands of No Child Left Behind and the reality of an increasingly disengaged student body, administrators and teachers are finding that they must continually find a balance between current practice and meeting the needs of a new breed of students. It's no panacea, but use of digital video in classrooms has the potential to help students learn more using a medium they value and like.

## ADDITIONAL RESOURCES

In addition to the resources cited above, you can learn more by accessing these online resources:

"Video Goes to School, Part 2," in eSchoolNews Online: http://www.eschoolnews.com/news/showStorysr.cfm?ArticleID=5641 (May 2005). Part two of a three-part report on video in classrooms, this article focuses specifically on video streaming. Free registration required.

eSchoolNews Online, Video Resource Center: http://www.eschool news.com/vrc/. Articles, product showcases, library links, and more. Free registration required.

Multimedia Seeds Web, Exploring Audio and Video Collections: http://eduscapes.com/seeds/stream.html. An explanation of streaming video and links to a number of resources.

National Center for Education Statistics: http://nces.ed.gov/. This federal entity collects and analyzes data related to education in the United States and around the world.

Northwest Regional Educational Laboratory, School Change Collaborative: http://www.nwrel.org/scpd/natspec/coldev.html. Founded in 1996, this group strives to help schools involve students as they work toward school reform.

# QUESTIONS FOR DISCUSSION

1. Do you agree that use of video enhances instruction? Explain.

2. What are the benefits and drawbacks of using digital video in the classroom?

3. Which digital format (DVD or streaming video) would you prefer to adopt at your site? Explain.

4. Describe the kind of professional development teachers at your site/district would need to successfully implement use of digital video.

5. What steps would your site/district need to take to ensure that the infrastructure could handle video streaming?

6. Review the 10 tips for using video. Which is most important? Explain.

7. Based upon your own experience, what other tip(s) would you add to the list?

# 12

## *Distance Learning in the K–12 Learning Environment*

Home study courses first became available in the United States as early as 1873. Using mail service to send and receive materials, early instructors were providing educational opportunities to women living in and near Boston. As communication technology has grown, so have the possibilities for distance education. Today it's possible for students of all ages and all walks of life to study with instructors anywhere in the world using an Internet-connected computer. How is your school capitalizing on these new capabilities?

Do you remember correspondence courses? Beginning in the 1920s, these print-based distance learning classes were offered to adult learners by a variety of providers. Distance learning has continued to exist in various manifestations, and this approach to adult education is still found through programs offered by trade schools, universities, governmental agencies, and military training. Today, distance learning

SOURCE: *Today's School*, March/April 2002

opportunities are also provided on K–12 school campuses in several formats, although often not to the degree found in adult programs. One reason for this is that full-blown distance learning courses often require a level of self-direction many K–12 students do not yet possess. Other factors include teacher and parent support, accreditation concerns, and funding issues. What kinds of distance learning experiences are being offered to younger students?

Suppose that your mainstream academic program could be enhanced through communication with experts around the world who are willing to mentor students and assist in designing collaborative projects with multiple schools. Perhaps your district serves a handful of students who are housebound due to illness. It may be that yours is a small, remote district or a large, urban district not able to offer alternative education programs to students ranging from those who have been expelled to those who need to enroll in advanced placement courses beyond your current staffing capabilities. Or, perhaps your teachers need and want professional development opportunities, but with after school programs, Saturday school, and other committee and meeting responsibilities, no one has the time to travel to a local university or county office of education for additional training.

Each scenario above describes a situation where distance learning models are being used to meet student and staff needs in K–12 settings.

## WHAT IS DISTANCE LEARNING?

Distance learning opportunities are designed for situations where students and teachers are not in the same physical location, and they range from a single encounter to a full course of instruction. Once they were confined to print material and written correspondence, but as technologies have improved over the decades, so have communications options in distance learning. For example, video technologies—including taped lectures and video conferencing, along with telephone conferencing—enabled students and teachers separated by distance to interact more fully with each other. Today, using Internet technology capabilities that allow for self-paced instruction, e-mail contact, chat rooms, video or audio streaming, and other features, distance learning classes can be either synchronous (taking place in real time with students and teachers working simultaneously) or asynchronous (students and teachers working where and when they choose). As costs for various communications technologies continue to decrease and access increases to high-speed connections that allow students and schools to both receive and transmit professional-quality digital video, the possibilities for quality distance learning experiences grow dramatically.

Depending upon the circumstances and needs of your educational community, you may want to take advantage of existing distance learning opportunities and courses by incorporating special events into your curriculum or by making parents and students aware of course availability and assisting in the enrollment process. On the other hand, you may need to take a more active role in course design and offerings. Each approach requires time and commitment on the part of your staff.

## CHOOSING EXISTING DISTANCE LEARNING PROGRAMS

This option requires that you review existing courses and other distance learning opportunities to identify those that will meet student needs. In order to do this, you need to understand the elements of well-designed distance learning experiences. You will want to begin by doing some research. "What Makes a Good Online Course," an article written by Lee R. Alley and available online at www.centerdigitaled.com/converge/?pg=magstory&id=9054, is a good place to start. Another good resource both for research on distance learning and for models of successful distance learning is the Instructional Technology Council Web site, www.itcnetwork.org/, where you can access an online library of articles, reports, and resources.

Briefly, here are some questions to consider. Does the course or activity meet the educational goals for your particular students and can it accommodate their individual needs? Is the instructional provider accredited and are teachers fully credentialed? Next, consider the technologies that are used to achieve these goals. Do the selected technologies fit well with the goals of the course? Is the course accessible through a variety of technology platforms? While access to high-end equipment may facilitate content delivery, lower-end technologies including fax machines and telephones are also effective in a well-designed course. The third consideration is support. Is the teacher of the course readily accessible to students through e-mail, telephone, fax, or other means? Does the teacher work to develop an online class community? What are tuition costs and who will be responsible for paying them? Are the technologies needed for the course currently available to students?

In most K–8 situations, you will probably choose to begin with a subscription program such as TEAMS (http://teams.lacoe.edu). This project uses distance learning and classroom-based activities in content areas such as mathematics and language arts to combine on-site teaching with television programs and Internet-based activities. Extensive instructional support materials are available to subscribing classroom teachers.

At the high school level, consider collaborative projects, one-time events, and complete courses of study. For example, using a telephone and an Internet connection, astronomy students at our local high school recently worked with astronomers at Mt. Wilson Observatory without stepping off campus. This same high school offers online makeup courses through NovaNET to students who want to raise their grades but cannot fit another class into a full schedule. In addition to NovaNET (www .pearsondigital.com/#NN), some other resources for complete courses are class.com (www.class.com), and Apex Learning (www.apexlearning.com). Because high schools are subject to accreditation, also refer to the "Best Practices for Electronically Offered Degree and Certificate Programs," available online at www.wcet.info/resources/accreditation/Accrediting %20-%20Best%20Practices.pdf when researching and selecting distance learning courses for students.

Regardless of whether you use distance learning experiences to enhance classroom instruction or for complete courses of study, schools serving all grade levels have found that having an on-site facilitator—someone who oversees instructional materials and schedules, enrollment, and student progress in course completion—helps make the distance learning experience more meaningful.

## DESIGNING YOUR OWN COURSES

While it is more common at the college or university level, there may be instances where K–12 teachers decide to create their own distance learning courses to meet specific student needs. This second option requires even a greater commitment of time because you must design courses, provide teachers, and then actually offer the classes. Distance learning efforts on this scale are almost always beyond the scope of an individual school, requiring that you work as part of a consortium of schools through a district or county office in order to muster necessary resources. Florida Gulf Coast University offers Principles of Online Design at www.fgcu.edu/ onlinedesign/designDev.html. You can also refer to the Rubric for Online Instruction hosted by California State University, Chico at www.csuchico .edu/celt/roi/. Although these are postsecondary institutions, the principles for design still hold true.

## VIRTUAL SCHOOLS

There are now models for virtual schools, state-approved and accredited, where students complete most or all of their coursework online. Florida has offered a statewide virtual high school since 1997. Enrollment for the 2004–05 school year exceeded 33,000 students and more than 80 courses were taught, ranging from GED to AP. Kentucky opened its statewide virtual high school in 2000, offering courses to all high school students in the state as well as professional development opportunities to Kentucky teachers. The Western Pennsylvania Cyber Charter School for K–12 students opened five years ago. Now Pennsylvania has 12 cyber charter schools with more than 10,000 students enrolled. The cyber schools continue to raise controversy. Some educators fear that there may be problems with course content and that students who attend a virtual school exclusively miss out on important social interaction and teacher contact. Founders of these schools agree that potential problems exist, but are confident that most challenges can be addressed.

## STUDENT PERFORMANCE

Many teachers express a natural concern that students may not do as well academically in any distance learning situation. However, research done in 1989 and 1992 (Chute, Balthazar, & Poston, 1989; Task Force on Distance Education, 1992) indicates that often student performance is actually better because students are required to take more responsibility for their own learning. Reports from virtual high schools including those in Florida and Kentucky indicate that online AP students score higher on the AP exams than those students taking the course in a traditional setting. To learn more about student performance in distance learning settings, there are a number of organizations that offer information via the Internet. Three Web sites to visit are

- **US Distance Learning Association:** www.usdla.org
- **Distance Education at a Glance:** www.uidaho.edu/evo/distglan .html
- **Distance Educator.com:** www.distance-educator.com/

## PROFESSIONAL DEVELOPMENT

Various factors have increased the need for ongoing professional development for educators while decreasing the time available for them to participate in classes and workshops themselves. School administrators find themselves looking beyond classic professional development models to meet current staff needs. Distance learning may be the answer for some situations and some individuals.

Staff development providers agree that on-site professional development is more effective than leaving campus to attend a meeting elsewhere, but bringing someone on campus isn't always possible. Several providers are now using video conferencing to try to bridge this gap. Visit Pacific Bell's site at www.kn.pacbell.com/wired/vidconf/ideas.html to read more about video conferencing in general; then contact local county offices of education or universities to find out about video conferencing in your area.

Another distance learning option for teachers is online courses. Many universities, colleges, and other staff development providers now offer this option to their students. For example, the Distance Learning Project at Teachers College, Columbia University (www.tc-library.org/Supportfor Learners.asp) offers online professional development and graduate credit in educational technology, staff development, and cognitive studies. Two additional resources are the Institute of Computer Technology (www.ict .org/) and Classroom Connect (http://corporate.classroom.com/).

## HOW DO YOU INITIATE THE KIND OF CHANGE NECESSARY TO EFFECTIVELY INTEGRATE DISTANCE LEARNING?

Simply having information about distance learning isn't enough. While this innovation may provide tools that enable educators to move toward true technology-based instruction, no matter what the quality of the offerings, or how readily available they are to staff members, we will not see changes in student performance if teachers simply use the technology to streamline assignments, or don't choose to make changes in instructional practices at all.

Alan November (1998), currently senior partner with Educational Renaissance Planners, suggests that it is time for those involved in technology and education to challenge some basic assumptions and beliefs that no longer work in the classroom. He also states that we spend too much time and energy on technology planning and not enough time focusing on the quality of the information we can access using the technology or on the quality of the relationships we form with one another and students.

Before a school staff sits down to make decisions about choosing or developing distance learning courses, they must first agree that this is, in fact, what they want to do. It is important for teachers to discuss the kinds of communication and information they need to have available in order to provide an environment where students will develop lifelong learning skills. When the staff is able to articulate these needs, they will be able to identify the technologies that will help them reach their goals.

Taking the time to discuss educational issues first will help when it does come time to make decisions about distance learning. Specific areas that require consideration, and that will be more easily answered after establishing a foundation based on educational issues, include criteria to be used when selecting or designing courses and activities useful for students and teachers, preliminary training needed to help both teachers and students become more discerning technology users, and the purposes behind using various technology-based tools.

This is not a process that occurs during one staff meeting, and it is necessary to guard against "analysis paralysis," but the time devoted to reflection and discussion is time well spent in the long run. Each discussion helps the staff better focus on what it is they really need: once that's been established, you then tackle issues of how to go about getting there.

It's easy to fall into the trap of implementing first and asking questions later. This has been particularly true with technology use, where programs have been adopted and then people have found themselves dealing with implementation issues. Although you cannot anticipate every possible problem that may arise, additional upfront planning for how you want to realize your established goals can be helpful in avoiding some roadblocks.

Look at the big picture. In addition to immediate budget needs, systemic change in technology based teaching practice requires ongoing support in a variety of areas including hardware compatibility; technical support and maintenance; staff development; parent education; ongoing costs for subscriptions, class tuition, and Internet access; and instructional program evaluation. A clearly articulated plan can be used to establish policies and procedures that will enable you to achieve your goals.

This is an exciting time in education. The possibilities for providing meaningful, highly successful instructional programs for students and families are there. Technology offers some of the tools we need to create and sustain these programs. It's up to us to make the decision to take full advantage of what is being offered.

# REFERENCES

Alley, L. R. (2001). What makes a good online course? *Converge, 4*(11), 50–53.

Chute, A., Balthazar, L., & Poston, C. (1989). Learning from teletraining. In M. Moore (Ed.), *Readings in Distance Learning and Instruction.* University Park: Penn State University Press.

Heerema, D. L., & Rogers, R. L. (2001). Avoiding the quality/quantity trade-off in distance education. *T.H.E. Journal, 29*(5), 14–21.

November, A. (1998, February). Creating a new culture of teaching and learning. [Online article based on a presentation at the 1998 Asilomar Symposium on Standards, Students, and Success, Asilomar, California]. http://www.a november.com/articles/asilomar.html

Task Force on Distance Education. (1992, November). *Report of the task force on distance education.* University Park: Penn State University Press.

The Web-Based Education Commission. (2000). *The power of the internet for learning: Moving from promise to practice.* Washington, DC: Author.

# ADDITIONAL RESOURCES

In addition to the resources cited above, you can learn more by accessing these online resources:

Education Commission of the States: www.ecs.org/. Use the site's search feature to find a number of recent resources on distance learning and cyber schools.

GlobalEducator.com: www.globaled.com/. The focus is higher education, but secondary-level educators can learn a great deal from the articles posted here.

Illinois Online Network: www.ion.illinois.edu/resources/. Case studies, articles, tutorials, and blogs related to distance learning.

Michigan Virtual High School: www.mivhs.org/. Explore online resources available to high school students in Michigan.

North Central Regional Educational Laboratory, Virtual Schools and E-Learning in K–12 Environments: Emerging Policy and Practice: http://www.ncrel.org/policy/pubs/html/pivol11/apr2002.htm. An overview of the issues and links to resources and research.

## QUESTIONS FOR DISCUSSION

1. What types of distance learning opportunities are currently offered to students in your site/district? Explain.

2. What types of distance learning opportunities are currently offered to teachers and staff members in your site/district? Explain.

3. Based upon your experience, discuss the benefits and drawbacks of distance learning for students.

4. Based upon your experience, discuss the benefits and drawbacks of distance learning for teachers and other staff members.

5. In your opinion, what kinds of student learning experiences lend themselves best to distance learning?

6. In your opinion, what kinds of teacher and staff member learning experiences lend themselves best to distance learning?

7. Do your students have the option of enrolling in a virtual school? Why, or why not?

# 13

# Project-Based Learning

## Technology Makes It Realistic!

In *Windows on the Future* (Corwin Press, 2001), Ian Jukes and Ted McCain describe the kinds of skills today's students must develop to compete successfully in a global economy. Large, predictable corporations are being replaced by small, flexible businesses where employees must be able to work with colleagues to identify problems, pose solutions, and the follow through to resolution. Project-based learning experiences are a perfect vehicle for encouraging students to learn these skills. This column explores project-based learning and how technology can be used to simplify classroom implementation.

Students in a fourth-grade class will be studying the history of their region. Developing an understanding of the importance of transportation, commerce, and geography is included in the standards related to this topic. In addition to using the textbook, their teacher decides to expand this topic into a multidisciplinary, standards-based unit dealing with problem solving and real-life issues. The crucial role played by the railroad in

---

SOURCE: *Today's Catholic Teacher*, April 2005

the early development of this community is an important piece of local history. Coincidentally, the old train depot, built in the late nineteenth century, is threatened with demolition, and community opinion about the building's future is sharply divided. People are writing letters, signing petitions, and even forming an information picket line outside the depot.

The teacher asks her students what they know about the controversy and why they think it's such an important issue for the community. Some students have seen the picketing, but they don't understand why people care about an old, dilapidated building. Together the teacher and students decide to learn about the depot, find out why people have such strong feelings about it, and formulate recommendations about what should happen to the building.

Over the next two months, students work in small groups. Their research addresses academic standards in history, geography, economics, mathematics, and language arts. They learn to use a Web browser's advanced search features to conduct research, a word processor to write business letters and reports, a spreadsheet to create charts and graphs, and a multimedia presentation program for their final product. Students interview community members, take digital photos of the depot during a field trip, invite the mayor to make a presentation, and communicate with railroad officials and history buffs via e-mail. At the end of their investigation, each group creates a multimedia presentation explaining their solution to the problem. Parents, community members, and fellow students are invited to attend the presentations and provide feedback. The presentations are posted on the class Web site for review and comment by the community.

This is an example of project-based learning (PBL), an instructional approach that has captured the interest of many educators over the last 25 years. Until recently, issues of management and resources made it difficult for most teachers to implement PBL in their classrooms. However, advances in various technologies and Web-based resources, along with increased classroom access to technology, make PBL a realistic option today.

## WHAT IS PROJECT-BASED LEARNING?

There are varying definitions for PBL, but they include certain common characteristics. In this approach to instruction, teachers and groups of students strive to

- Identify a real-world problem
- Develop a directing or guiding question about the problem
- Investigate the issues
- Formulate a solution
- Create artifacts related to the solution and based upon the investigation

- Present the solution to others
- Assess student work throughout the project
- Reflect on accomplishments

Well-designed PBL activities are

- Standards-based
- Tied directly to the curriculum
- Multidisciplinary
- Open-ended
- Conducted over a period of time

PBL finds its roots in two important advances over the last 25 years. The first is our growing understanding of how people learn. Students who become active participants in their own learning increase their academic performance and believe that schooling is relevant to them.

The second advance is our recent plunge into the Information Age. Simple factual knowledge is no longer enough to guarantee success in the working world. Now, in addition to the traditional three Rs, our graduates are expected to be able to identify and solve problems, work well in small task-oriented groups, deal with large amounts of information, plan and carry out multiple tasks with limited supervision, self-assess the quality of their work, and reflect on their experiences to improve the quality of future work. The PBL approach, when used properly, addresses the needs to engage students in their learning and to provide opportunities for them to develop skills for a successful work life.

Teachers and students assume new roles when engaged in PBL. The teacher sometimes acts as a director, managing the logistics of a project such as arranging for a field trip or providing direct instruction in research skills. At other times, the teacher becomes a facilitator, helping students find resources or resolve problems that arise in group work. Students must be taught to work collaboratively, learning to take responsibility for task completion and engaging in the give-and-take required for effective group work. In addition, students must master twenty-first-century skills such as literacy in technology, information, and media.

## HOW DOES PBL DIFFER FROM TRADITIONAL PROJECTS?

Good teachers have always encouraged their students to engage in projects that allow them to apply what they've learned. However, PBL classrooms place greater emphasis on projects and their place in daily instructional activities. In more traditional settings, project assignments such as Science Fair or History Day are often viewed as fun add-ons—something students complete individually after their other work is done, often outside the school day. Or projects such as state reports and career notebooks are assigned using strict, predetermined guidelines. This leaves little or no room for student creativity in planning how they will approach the assignment or design their final project.

In a PBL activity, the project is a critical part of the instructional day, not something accomplished in the evening, on weekends, or during Friday afternoons. This does not mean that teachers abandon direct instruction. Most basic skills must be specifically taught before they can be applied in other settings. But it does mean that teachers intentionally identify those times when PBL activities can be used to help students apply the skills they've learned in a real-world context, and build them into the regular instructional day.

## WHERE DOES TECHNOLOGY FIT IN?

There are three potential roadblocks to successful design and implementation of PBL activities. First, the amount of work required is far greater than for lessons based solely on textbooks. Second, students must be able to work independently as they conduct in-depth research, manage the information they have found, create products, and present their findings. Finally, PBL activities often include communicating with people off-site: other teachers and students, parents, community members, and area experts.

Various technologies address these challenges and make the process manageable for both teachers and students. Teachers may use application software and Web-based tools to design a project and deal with implementation logistics. The Internet provides access to a multitude of resources as well. Students use tools such as word processors, spreadsheets, databases, and multimedia presentation programs to work with information, while the Internet provides access to real-time data and a wealth of information. Finally, electronic communication via e-mail, videoconferencing, and online communities offers teachers and students opportunities to communicate with people outside the classroom. Below are some very helpful Web-based resources.

**edutopia:** www.glef.org. Less-experienced teachers may want to learn more about PBL before attempting to design a project on their own. This George Lucas Foundation Web site offers a free professional development module that explains the basics through readings, a PowerPoint presentation, and video clips. More-experienced teachers may want to visit this site to review the project-based learning topic area for ideas and examples.

**PBLnet:** www.pblnet.org. Want to find ideas for projects and Web-based resources to use with students? This WestEd site is a good place to start.

The primary focus is upper elementary and middle school, but teachers of other grade levels will also find helpful information here. Exemplary Projects spotlights several examples of PBL activities. The Design Challenge Database can be used to find ideas for projects by grade level, theme, activity format, project duration, and other criteria. The Design Resource Database offers access to online resources for PBL by resource type and grade level.

**bobpearlman.org, Project-Based Learning:** www.bobpearlman.org/BestPractices/PBL.htm. Bob Pearlman, experienced educator and consultant, has assembled a list of links to exemplary projects on this Web site. Be sure to check out the student work samples as well.

**Project-Based Learning, What Is It?** http://pblchecklist.4teachers.org. Concerned about managing and tracking activities? Visit this site, sponsored by the High Plains Regional Technology in Education Consortium, to review their free, Web-based PBL tools for teachers and students. Teachers can use Assign-a-Day, a Web-based calendar to create and monitor schedules. TrakStar allows teachers and students to organize annotated lists of online resources. ThinkTank is a research organizer for students in grades 3–8 and can be used in conjunction with NoteStar to keep research notes organized. CasaNotes offers templates for letters and forms teachers may need to create to send home. Use RubiStar, QuizStar, and PBL Checklists to create assessment tools. Web Worksheet Wizard makes it easy for teachers to create Web pages for classroom use.

Start small and expand your ideas as your comfort level increases. Many PBL activities originate in social studies or science and incorporate other content areas as appropriate. A good rule of thumb is to remember that the purpose of the activity is to cover a topic in depth, not to spread yourself and your students too thin. Give PBL a try! You and your students will reap many benefits.

## ADDITIONAL RESOURCES

In addition to the resources cited above, you can learn more by access these online resources:

Apple Learning Interchange., Teaching Methods: Project-Based Learning: http://ali.apple.com/ali_sites/deli/exhibits/1000328/Project-Based_Learning.html. Links to resources, examples, and video clips of students engaged in project-based learning.

Global Schoolhouse, Global SchoolNet: http://www.globalschoolnet.org/GSH/index.html. Students, teachers, parents, and community members may use this site for collaboration, project development, publishing, etc.

iEARN, International Education and Resource Network: http://www.iearn.org/. This site enables teachers and students to participate in learning projects that use the Internet and other technologies.

"Projects: Road Ahead (Project-Based Learning)," at ISTE Research, http://www.iste.org/Content/NavigationMenu/Research/Reports/The_Road_Ahead_Background_Papers_1997_/Project-Based_Learning.htm (1997). A draft of a report that was prepared for the National Education Association (NEA).

Oracle Education Foundation, ThinkQuest: http://www.thinkquest.org/. Students work in teams to explore a variety of relevant topics. Previous ThinkQuests are archived here as well.

## QUESTIONS FOR DISCUSSION

1. Define project-based learning.

2. What are the similarities and differences between activities designed for direct instruction and those designed for project-based learning?

3. What are the benefits and drawbacks to project-based learning?

4. How is project-based learning currently implemented at your site, or in your district?

5. How does access to technology relate to implementation of project-based learning?

6. Describe how teachers at your site/district could use the technology currently available to them to implement project-based learning.

7. In your opinion, what role should project-based learning play in today's classroom? Explain.

# PART III

## *Providing a Reliable Infrastructure*

An unreliable infrastructure is one of the first things educators mention when explaining why technology is not being used in instruction. The chapters in this section spotlight a number of issues administrators must address to correct this problem.

# 14

# *Managing Total Cost of Ownership*

While it's discouraging to visit schools with no visible technology program, it's even more disheartening to tour a school where technology is available but not used. Whether it's aging unreliable equipment, incompatibility issues, a lack of professional development, or another challenge, this disuse often relates directly back to a failure to plan for total cost of ownership. In order to create an environment that supports effective technology implementation, administrators must understand and plan for all elements of total cost of ownership. This chapter will help you get started.

My 22-year-old daughter, soon to be a college graduate, decided recently she wanted to purchase her first new car. She'd found a model she liked, saved the cash for the down payment, and was ready to go to a car lot to make a deal. Needing a cosigner, she came to me with her plan. Her answers to a few questions showed that

SOURCE: *Today's School*, November/December 2003

she needed to do some additional research. Yes, she had decided on an amount she could afford as a monthly payment, but hadn't realized the difference in cost between a three-year loan and a four- or five-year loan. She knew that her car insurance premium would increase, but didn't understand that the kind of car she purchased would directly impact the new premium amount. She also had not thought to consider factors such as mileage, maintenance, or the life expectancy of the car she wanted based on its performance record. After doing more homework she selected a more affordable and reliable car, then made her purchase. This was her first real experience with the concept of *total cost of ownership* (TCO), and she found that understanding initial and ongoing costs, both obvious and hidden, made a difference in what car she decided to buy.

School administrators are faced with the same kind of decision-making process when purchasing various technologies to support student instruction. However, just like my daughter, they often don't realize that they need to think beyond the initial purchase price of the equipment. This is particularly important for administrators who operate in a setting where the school district may assume few or none of the additional costs. What are the hidden or ongoing costs of technology, and how does a TCO-savvy administrator anticipate and manage them?

## IT BEGINS WITH TEAMWORK

Successfully tackling all the issues surrounding TCO requires that administrators work closely with other campus decision makers because it often requires that spending patterns be changed or purchasing choices redefined. When this type of decision is perceived as being top-down, it's generally not well received by teachers, so you need a good base of staff support. The job is too big for one or two people to handle alone, and involving all staff members in the process can bog things down to the point that no productive decisions are made. Start with a group respected by the staff, such as the leadership team or technology committee.

Provide an overview of the concept of TCO to the group. The Consortium for School Networking (CoSN) hosts a site that offers all the background information you need to share with campus leaders. Called "Taking TCO to the Classroom," and accessible at http://classroomtco .cosn.org, the Resources and Publications & Tools areas offer links to articles, white papers, and a PowerPoint slide show that explain the elements of TCO.

Once the group has a basic understanding of TCO issues, begin applying this knowledge to technology-supported instruction at the school site. Although there is crossover and things are not always clear-cut, it is helpful to think of costs in two categories: initial and ongoing. Both categories include obvious and less obvious, or hidden, costs. Initial costs include the price of hardware, peripherals, software, installation, and professional development to get staff up to speed with a new technology. Ongoing costs are the dollars that must be invested to keep equipment up and running and to keep staff up-to-date on effective use of the equipment. Hidden costs are all the additional dollars, usually unanticipated and unbudgeted, that are spent to successfully implement a new technology, and to keep technologies up and running. Schools that do not recognize and plan for hidden costs usually have less effective implementation of technology-supported instruction.

While some folks jump to solutions at this point, I find it's more effective to spend some additional time with the committee to talk about the kinds of hidden costs that may be incurred in both initial and ongoing spending. It's helpful to use a series of questions as a foundation for discussion. The questions identify points where hidden costs may arise and also assist the committee in recognizing current site practices that avoid or lead to hidden costs in both initial and ongoing expenditures. Once the committee has reviewed practices that might lead to higher costs, it's time to discuss more specifics about what those costs actually are, as well as strategies to manage them.

Based upon my work with schools and districts, I have developed two documents that can be used to stimulate discussion about hidden costs that arise initially and then as ongoing issues. Both documents are available on my Web site at www.sjbrooks-young.com/id13.html. Click on each document title ("TCO—Initial Hidden Costs" and "TCO—Ongoing Costs") to download. For the sake of simplicity, the forms discussed here focus on computer purchases; however, the questions can be modified to address various kinds of technologies.

## INITIAL HIDDEN COSTS

In general, there are six areas where hidden costs may be initially generated. These unexpected costs may be incurred due to the type of hardware selected, the peripherals required for implementation, the chosen location for the new equipment, installation of the equipment, the software selected for implementation, and the level of professional development needed. For example, choosing a desktop system because it is inexpensive may be a mistake if it is incompatible with existing equipment or if you need to purchase additional memory to make it capable of running the software to be used. Planning an online research center in a building on the edge of the campus may be a pricey venture by the time you factor in the cost of network connectivity.

| TCO—Initial Hidden Costs | | | |
|---|---|---|---|
| **Total Cost of Ownership: Computer Hardware** | | | |
| **Ask yourself** | **Yes** | **No** | **Don't know** |
| Is the system being considered compatible with existing equipment? | | | |
| Can the new system support your needs with its current specifications (i.e., enough memory, CD/DVD RW drive)? | | | |
| Is the manufacturer reliable? | | | |
| Is the warranty sufficient for your needs? | | | |
| Does the system have an acceptable performance record? | | | |
| Is the price affordable? | | | |
| Additional questions: | | | |

The purpose of the "TCO—Initial Hidden Costs" checklist is to identify instances where hidden costs might be generated through decisions made when new technology is purchased. The checklist consists of a series of questions related to the six hidden cost areas identified above. Each question is answered "Yes," "No," or "Don't Know." Although purchasing and installing new equipment and software always generates costs, hidden costs are less likely when the answer to a question is "Yes," while responses of "No" or "Don't Know" alerts the person completing the checklist that hidden or unanticipated costs may be involved. These items should be researched more fully to identify any additional costs. The point is not necessarily to answer each question "Yes," but rather to anticipate decisions that may include an additional cost. A sample from the first section of the hidden costs checklist appears here.

While the questions in the checklist may be applied to future purchases, use them initially to identify what factors are or are not important at your site. The first question addresses compatibility with existing equipment. Think about your most recent computer purchase. Was compatibility considered? Why or why not? Is it important to you that all systems be compatible with one another? What costs might arise when systems are incompatible? Continue through the remaining questions. Talking about these issues will help the committee when the time comes to establish TCO management strategies. For example, the committee may decide that compatibility is important, and, as a result, decide to establish basic specifications for all computers purchased.

## ONGOING COSTS

Prior to the availability of E-Rate and other funds that enabled schools to acquire large amounts of technology fairly quickly, ongoing costs, both obvious and hidden, were not given much thought. Now that schools have invested large amounts of money in technology, we realize that it takes much more than the initial investment to ensure that the technology is dependable and being used well. A study conducted by MIT (Rothstein & McKnight, "Technology and Cost Models of K–12 Schools on the National Information Infrastructure," 1996) suggests that ongoing costs are one-third to one-half of the initial investment, depending upon the complexity of the technology in place. In other words, for every $100 spent on technology, schools spend (or need to spend) another $33 to $50 *per year* to support the technology.

Where do these costs come from? There are seven general areas where ongoing costs, both obvious and hidden, arise. These areas are maintenance/technical support, supplies/components, software, utilities/telecommunications, professional development, recycling/retrofitting, and monitoring and evaluation. For example, it was once assumed that professional development focused on basic computer usage was enough to enable teachers to figure out how to use technology effectively in the classroom. Research and experience now tell us this is not the case. Teachers need ongoing, increasingly sophisticated instruction in how to use technology well in their classrooms. Evaluation and monitoring of the technology used is also costly. Even the time you take with your committee in reviewing TCO issues is a hidden cost, probably not covered in your current budget!

The purpose of the "TCO—Ongoing Costs" tables is to identify those costs currently included in your budget, the percentage of the budget allocated for the costs, those costs not budgeted for, and how the unbudgeted services are currently provided (Hint: these are probably your hidden ongoing costs). The tables, one for each of the seven areas listed above, consist of a series of questions that can be answered "Yes" or "No." When a question is answered "Yes," you are asked to identify how much of the budget is currently allocated to cover the cost. This helps you determine if the amount is appropriate. When the answer is "No," you are asked to state how the service is provided. This helps identify services that cost money, even when not included in the official budget. These items should be researched more fully to identify the true cost involved.

A sample table from the first section of the ongoing costs checklist appears here.

| TCO—Ongoing Costs | | | | |
|---|---|---|---|---|
| **Total Cost of Ownership: Maintenance** | | | | |
| **Ask yourself**<br>**Don't know** | **Yes** | **% of**<br>**Budget** | **No** | **We provide**<br>**this service by** |
| Routine maintenance for computer systems and peripherals? | | | | |
| Regular upgrades for hardware (i.e., additional memory)? | | | | |
| Making repairs on nonfunctioning equipment? | | | | |
| Troubleshooting? | | | | |
| Ongoing technical support? | | | | |
| Additional questions: | | | | |
| Total % of budget currently allocated for maintenance: | | | | |

## MANAGEMENT STRATEGIES

Once the committee has a clear understanding of hidden and ongoing costs, they are in a position to make recommendations about how to manage your site's TCO expenses. It's important to understand that low TCO costs are not necessarily an indicator that technology is being managed effectively. It may mean that teachers and students are not working in a well-supported environment. For example, if maintenance and support costs are only five percent of your budget, your equipment is likely not receiving the basic attention required to keep it functioning dependably. CoSN's Taking TCO to the Classroom site also hosts a free online tool schools may use to project TCO costs. Found at http://classroomtco.cosn .org/gartner_intro.html, this Web-based survey can help you establish your site's TCO.

It's important to think about making purchases you can afford to support fully. Experience shows that teachers and students do not benefit from equipment that isn't working because it hasn't been maintained properly. Teachers shy away from using technologies they don't understand, particularly when there is no visible professional development support system in place. Once you've identified a use for technology, based upon its potential to support student performance, you need to ensure that you can afford to implement the program well. Below are some common strategies used by schools.

**Standardize hardware purchases.** Although it's tempting to buy the least expensive technology at the time you want to write a purchase order, this can lead to a variety of hidden costs, both initially and ongoing. The cheapest hardware may not have the capabilities needed to implement the instructional program. For example, an inexpensive digital camera may also require a memory card before multiple students can use it. A computer system may not have enough memory to run the instructional software you have selected. Standardizing the hardware you purchase not only saves on initial costs, but also on ongoing costs for maintenance and repair. Technical support staff cannot be expected to keep their skills up to par on every type of hardware available. However, it is reasonable to expect that they can support a limited list of hardware. Standardization also enables you to target professional development activities for depth as well as initial introductory activities.

**Standardize software purchases.** Schools generally identify specific curricula for content area instruction. Teachers may supplement the basic materials, but not substitute a completely different curriculum on their own. Instructional software can be standardized using the same model. This often results in an initial savings when multiple copies of the same program are purchased and makes it possible to provide appropriate professional development training using programs everyone can access. Ongoing costs for support, upgrades, and further training are also reduced. Just as support staff cannot be expected to repair a grab bag of hardware, they cannot fully support a lengthy list of different software programs. Simply tracking subscriptions and updates can become a full-time job when limits are not set. Teachers also need to know that help is available when they have difficulty operating a program or when they want additional training in using a piece of software. These needs can be met when support staff can target their energies.

Some schools deal with standardization of hardware and software by developing a policy that identifies what *will* be supported and stating clearly that when individual teachers choose to make purchases off the list they will also be responsible for additional initial and ongoing costs.

**Set aside a predetermined amount of money for each system purchased.** Some schools handle TCO by setting aside a predetermined amount of money for every hardware dollar spent. The figure varies, but is based upon an analysis of overall TCO costs. If you have funds that can be carried over, the money can be encumbered at the time the purchase is made. Be careful not to exceed the carryover limit. Another approach is to take TCO dollars off the top as you plan each year's new budget. Again, this figure is typically based upon the initial cost of the hardware and then needs to be available each year of the projected life of the equipment.

**Purchase extended warranties.** Buying extended warranties increases initial costs, but some schools see a tremendous savings in ongoing maintenance and repair costs. A hidden cost in making this purchase is the time it takes for a staff member to register hardware and software and then monitor warranty expiration dates. Using this approach may also slow down repair schedules, depending upon the manufacturer.

**Leverage current funding streams.** Title II, Part D funding requires that 25 percent of the money be used for professional development. There are similar requirements with other funding sources. Use these requirements to assist you in covering ongoing costs of professional development. By integrating technology use throughout all content-area in-service trainings, you not only offer teachers training they need, but can also offer the technology training within the context of instruction and curriculum. Explore regulations for other federal and state categorical funds to see what other kinds of initial and ongoing costs may be covered.

**Lease equipment.** This approach works best when you have guaranteed income over a period of time. Manufacturers offer leasing programs, but you can sometimes get a better deal through companies that specialize in equipment leasing.

**Consider alternative technologies.** This can be dicey because alternatives may not be as well tested as more traditional technologies, but that doesn't mean they don't merit research and perhaps even a pilot program. Alternatives such as thin-client networks, PC blades (a new technology used successfully with servers and now being brought to the desktop level), handheld computers, or application service providers (companies that make software available on a subscription basis) may reduce initial and overall TCO costs.

**Implement in stages.** You don't need to do everything at once. Some schools spread costs out over time by staggering implementation by grade level, department, or content area.

**Schedule replacements.** Just like textbooks, technologies should be replaced on an ongoing basis. A school can set up a cycle for hardware and software replacement that includes the costs of upgrades (as long as they are practical), the cost of equipment disposal, and the costs of replacing equipment including retrofitting for new equipment demands.

Ignoring it won't reduce the impact of TCO. Take a proactive stance to assist stakeholders in making sound decisions about managing these costs to ensure successful program implementation. Your staff and students will reap many benefits from well-supported technology-based programs.

## ADDITIONAL RESOURCES

In addition to the resources cited above, you can learn more by accessing these online resources:

IAETE: K12 TCO Calculator, v2.0: http://129.71.174.252/tcov2/. Use this Web-based tool to project TCO costs between three and five years out. Supporting documents are also available.

International Society for Technology in Education, Technology Support Index: http://tsi.iste.org/. A framework and tool districts can use to begin a discussion about how to manage TCO.

National Clearinghouse for Educational Facilities, Resource Lists: Technology Integration 2000–2005: http://www.edfacilities.org/rl/technologyII.cfm. An annotated Webliography of articles, books, and links related to integrating technology use into school facilities.

"Investing in Palm Handhelds: Understanding Total Cost of Ownership," in *PalmPower Magazine Enterprise Edition:* http://www.palm powerenterprise.com/issuesprint/issue200109/tco.html (n.d.). This article explores TCO issues for handheld computers.

Sustaining Technology Through Time: http://www.sonoma.edu/users/p/phelan/504/sustain.htm. This online course activity helps educators understand the basics of TCO.

# QUESTIONS FOR DISCUSSION

1. Complete the Initial Hidden Costs worksheet. What did you learn about your site's/district's current strategies for anticipating hidden costs?

2. Complete the Ongoing Costs worksheet. What did you learn about your site's/district's current strategies for planning for ongoing costs for technology?

3. Describe your site/district budget practices related to TCO.

4. Standardization of hardware and software purchases is a common approach used to manage TCO. This does save money, but also may have unintended consequences that inhibit use of new technologies. In your opinion, what are effective strategies for striking a balance in this area?

5. Leasing equipment rather than making outright purchases is increasingly popular as a cost-saving measure. Has your district adopted this practice? Why, or why not?

6. What steps do you take in planning for equipment replacement and recycling?

7. What changes can you make in your budgeting practices to better plan for TCO?

# 15

*Tech-Ready Facilities*

> Architects, contractors, and maintenance workers are not trained educators. And yet, those who work in school settings make instructional decisions every day. Students and teachers are the beneficiaries when proactive administrators ensure that they are included during every phase of planning and building for remodels or new construction. This chapter provides an overview of some of the issues that may arise.

To meet increased demands for ready access to instructional technology, school technology plans now commonly include provisions to provide multiple computer systems and at least one printer in every classroom. However, classrooms and other instructional areas are often not well suited for this level of technology installation, even when a facility is relatively new or has recently undergone remodeling. While most leaders realize they need to resolve infrastructure issues such as access to adequate electricity and network connectivity, there are additional factors that must be addressed when increasing student and teacher access to technology in classrooms. Consider the following examples.

A K–8 school recently underwent a multimillion-dollar renovation. This technology magnet school now boasts five to six computers in each

---

SOURCE: *Today's School*, September/October 2004

classroom and a large lab with 30 workstations. But there are structural issues with the lab. While there is ample room for the workstations, four floor-to-ceiling support columns in the center of the room block lines of vision, making it impossible for students who are using computers near the columns to see the instructor or images projected at the front of the room.

An elementary school upgraded the electrical system and network connectivity in each classroom. As a cost-saving measure, multiple outlets and drops were installed in one interior wall in each classroom. To safely connect computers and other peripherals, all equipment must be located along this one wall. Several problems have arisen due to this configuration. Glare from windows on the opposite wall makes it difficult for students to read their monitor screens. Teachers who want to have students work in small groups find there isn't enough room for each group to use a computer simultaneously. Also, this wall was originally the front of the classroom; although furniture has been rearranged, the whiteboard and large monitor have not yet been moved and are now awkward to use.

These problems are not insurmountable, but they do reflect the need to think carefully about what constitutes a tech-ready classroom, and they highlight the importance of working closely with facilities planners and contractors.

## HOW WILL THE TECHNOLOGY BE USED TO SUPPORT LEARNING AND TEACHING?

Individual teachers' instructional styles and philosophies about technology integration are critical factors in successful implementation of technology-supported instruction. Before retrofitting or bringing in new equipment, it's important for each teacher to think about how he or she regularly provides instruction and how technology use will support or enhance that approach. Teachers who rely heavily on lecture with individual follow-up activities will want a different configuration for the technology in their classrooms than teachers who expect students to engage frequently in online group work. Teachers who have lab activities associated with their content areas will have different technology needs than teachers who do not. Teachers who require students to conduct regular research will have specific configuration needs for both the classroom and the library/media center. Although it may be argued that all teachers should immediately step up their use of technology-supported instruction when access is increased, it's more realistic to recognize that teachers must be supported at their current skill levels and then encouraged to expand use over time in an environment that will support that shift. This level of flexibility can be made available by considering future expansion to accommodate teacher growth in technology use and to anticipate needs for increased access due to better, less expensive technology.

Prior to meeting with the facilities planner, staff members must be able to articulate their needs clearly. Ask teachers to describe their instructional strategies and how they will use technology to support or enhance these approaches. They also need to think about how they will use available classroom space to house the technology and provide other working areas. What furniture will be needed? What would be the ideal configuration? Where will equipment be placed? How and when will the equipment be used? In middle and high schools it also may be appropriate to host student focus groups to gather feedback about how they'd like to use technology.

## MAKING THE BEST USE OF INSTRUCTIONAL SPACE

Once the staff has a good handle on how they want technology to be used to support instruction, they should thoroughly examine existing or planned instructional spaces to determine what issues may be posed by physical constraints. Facilities planners estimate that a single desktop computer or printer requires 15 to 20 square feet of classroom space. Most classrooms are able to accommodate a teaching station placed on the teacher's desk, and then two or three spaces for a combination of desktop systems and printers. But five computers and a printer take up an additional 90 to 120 square feet. Finding that space in every classroom necessitates a careful assessment in order to identify strategies to maximize that use.

Facilities planners and contractors understand how to increase the use of space and employ cost-effective measures, but they're not educators. Staff members must bring their instructional and classroom management expertise to the table and take an active role in planning, whether the goal is to maximize existing space, remodel a facility, or design a new building. Here are some steps that can be taken by educators when considering potential facilities issues:

1. Carefully review the architectural plans for the building(s). Whether the plans are for the existing facility, a new structure, or a remodel, each staff member must look at the floor plans for his/her classroom and for common instruction areas, e.g., labs or the library/media center. Keeping in mind the amount of equipment planned for installation now as well as possible future expansion, the following questions should be asked:

   - **How are the classrooms and common areas configured?** The shape of the room, connecting space between classrooms, alcoves, and obstructions (e.g., support columns) all impact how space will be used for learning areas and traffic flow.

- **What sources of light are available in the classrooms and common instruction areas?** The size and location of windows and the type of fixtures used may cause glare on monitor screens.
- **Where are the electrical outlets and how many are available?** Due to safety considerations, at least two duplex outlets should be available for each workstation, and circuits should be equipped with surge protection. Freestanding workstations are more difficult to supply with power than workstations placed next to a wall.
- **What type of network connectivity is provided?** Again, unless wireless connectivity is available, freestanding workstations are more difficult to connect to the network than workstations placed next to a wall.
- **Is the space properly cooled for the amount of equipment to be installed?** One or two desktop computers have little or no impact on room temperature. However, five computers and a printer can require an additional ton of air-conditioning equipment per classroom.

2. Based upon this review, staff members should compare their descriptions of an ideal setting for technology use with the existing plans to identify potential problems. Some remedies will be easier to manage than others. For example, glare resulting from sunlight might be diminished by placing computers in another location, by tinting the window glass, or by installing antiglare screens on monitors. Purchasing battery-operated laptops that can be used anywhere in the room rather than stationary desktop units may solve some problems related to placement of workstations, although it may also be necessary to replace student desks with tables to accommodate laptops and other working materials and to permit small group work.

Other problems, such as placement of electrical outlets and network drops, selection of lighting fixtures, poor room configuration, or HVAC requirements, may require expensive modifications. These must be discussed with the facilities planner to identify practical solutions. However, although costs may be incurred through changes made during planning, they will almost certainly be less than the cost of redoing something during or after construction.

Today's tech-ready classrooms provide flexibility to accommodate a variety of instructional styles and changing technologies. These facilities maximize usage of existing space or provide additional space for workstations. Tech-ready facilities also take into account environmental factors including lighting, HVAC, appropriate furniture, and traffic patterns. It's important for school leaders to remember that no matter how well-designed a new building may appear or how comprehensive a remodel may be, the end-users—both staff and older students—must be involved in the planning process. While there are many talented facilities planners who bring a wealth of experience to the table, ultimately it's the end-user who must be able to explain his or her needs and plans for how technology use will be implemented, and then work with the planning team to develop strategies that will meet these needs.

## ADDITIONAL RESOURCES

You can learn more by accessing these online resources:

enGauge, Indicator: Technology-Ready Facilities: www.ncrel.org/ engauge/framewk/acc/facility/accfacin.htm. Although slightly dated, this site addresses many facilities issues administrators need to consider when planning technology-supported programs.

National Clearinghouse for Educational Facilities: www.edfacilities .org/. This site offers information about planning, designing, funding, building, improving, and maintaining schools. The Technology Education Resource List is especially helpful.

School Facilities.com: www.schoolfacilities.com/. Visit the Articles area of this Web site and click on the Technology link. You'll find several articles that address various issues related to facilities and technology in schools.

"School Facilities for the 21st Century, 12 Trends That School Facility Planners Need to Know About" in *School Business Affairs*, available online at http://asbointl.org/asbo/files/ccPageContentdocfilename 000754857432Decarticle.pdf (December 2001). This article identifies important trends that will impact school facility design.

*School Planning & Management* magazine: http://www.peterli.com/ spm/index.shtm. The article archive includes several articles related to technology-ready facilities.

## QUESTIONS FOR DISCUSSION

1. Describe an ideal setting for classroom technology use.

2. Explain how this ideal setting is, or is not, aligned with existing classrooms in your site/district.

3. Describe an ideal setting for a computer laboratory.

4. Explain how this ideal setting is, or is not, aligned with existing laboratories in your site/district.

5. This chapter draws a direct correlation between facilities design and teacher use of technology. In your experience, what steps must be taken to ensure that teachers are able to use technology without being constrained by issues with facility design?

6. How do administrators in your district ensure adequate communication with one another and outside contractors during remodeling and new construction projects?

7. Having read this chapter, how will you change the role you assume in your site's next remodel or construction project?

# 16

## Software and Networks

### The New Challenges

Is there ever a time when the need for network integrity and security supersedes instructional needs? Who makes that call in your school/district? This is a growing concern as the amount of equipment and level of connectivity continues to grow in schools and districts, and far too often it's a technician who is calling the shots. Administrators must make a point of staying on top of policies, procedures, and concerns related to infrastructure reliability and facilitating meaningful technology-based instruction.

A teacher who is a reluctant technology user finds a software program that is well aligned with her curriculum, easy to use, and compatible with the school network. She's eager to get it installed and use it with her students. Although she completed and submitted the proper paperwork, six months later she's still waiting for the program to be approved and installed. She covered the curriculum supported by the software three months ago. That spark of interest is now extinguished.

SOURCE: *Today's School*, May/June 2005

At another school, a teacher inadvertently crashes the entire network when he installs a program that is not compatible with the operating system. It takes days to identify the problem and correct it. In the meantime, no one at the site has computer access and teachers and office staff scramble to find alternate ways to deal with reports and technology-based activities.

In a third instance, a teacher learns that as a result of a new software standardization policy, a program he's used successfully will be removed from the network. He does not see how he can adapt any of the approved programs for his lessons, so he stops incorporating the use of software in his instructional units.

Those of us who have been in education for a while remember when we were grateful to find a software program that was even remotely applicable to the curriculum . . . and the funds to pay for it! With our standalone 64K computers that boasted single or dual five-inch floppy drives, we didn't worry about whether or not using a particular program would impact other technology users on campus. We also had little or no concern about compatibility, multistation licensing issues, or viruses. As a result, teachers had a high level of autonomy when it came to selecting and using educational software. Who would have imagined that one day we would be faced with the possibility of having to limit access to software in order to preserve the integrity of a computer network?

How are districts and individual schools dealing with these issues? My conversations with educators throughout the United States reveal that, while various approaches are being tried, most folks are not satisfied with the results. Teachers and administrators tell tales of limited or no access to software they want and need, while technicians report that it's nearly impossible to keep networks running smoothly given their limited time and resources. Here are three of the most commonly reported approaches, along with inherent problems and possible antidotes.

## SOFTWARE APPROVAL COMMITTEES

Districts using this model require that a centralized committee review new software before it is approved for classroom use. The rationale is that committee review will ensure that classroom software meets minimum standards both instructionally and technically.

**The reality**—This process bogs down for a number of reasons. Sometimes it's a scheduling issue. The committee cannot meet often enough to keep up with requests. Other times it's because committee membership does not include both educators and technicians or isn't really a committee at all because just one or two people are making the decisions. When this happens, several problems may arise. The group slows down the process to defer to nonmembers for input or makes decisions that need to be changed later due to curricular or technical concerns. Credibility questions surface if just one or two people make decisions and do not have backgrounds in both curriculum and technology. Often there is little accountability built into the decision-making process. There are no set procedures for scheduling timely reviews and communicating decisions. This means that teachers and administrators may wait months before hearing from the committee and then have no idea why a program is approved or rejected. The result is often an "us vs. them" situation where committee members believe that their work is not appreciated and staff view decisions as being unfair.

**Antidote**—The mission of the committee must be to find ways to meet both instructional and technical needs. Teachers and administrators will be more inclined to trust the judgment of the group when they know that several experts in both fields are considering the instructional merit and technical issues of each software program. Committee members must include curriculum and technical experts whose opinions are respected by staff. Committees must make decisions in a timely way. The group must establish and publish a regular meeting schedule and a timeline for reviewing and reporting results; and they must adhere to this plan. When a program is not approved, a clear explanation should be provided.

## LIMITED ADMINISTRATIVE RIGHTS

A limited number of people in the district are given the authority to install new programs. Sometimes just one person is chosen. The rationale is that when just a few people can install programs, there is less chance that unlicensed or infected programs will be added. Also, if there is a compatibility issue, it will be easier to find the source of the problem. This strategy may be used in conjunction with a review committee.

**The reality**—Most districts have limited technical staff. In cases where only one technician is granted the authority to install new programs districtwide, it is nearly impossible for this person to keep up with the demands, particularly when this is just one of many responsibilities assigned and when no preliminary evaluation for network compatibility has occurred. Teachers often wait months before they can use a new program. In worst-case situations, the software is never used because the technician simply doesn't have the time to make it work.

Even in situations where one person at each school site has the authority to install software, time and limited expertise are problematic. Few sites are able to hire full-time technicians, so software installation becomes a side job done by a staff member who has other full-time responsibilities. There are also increased problems with compatibility and security, particularly when no preliminary review is done and when the individual is not a trained technician.

**Antidote**—Networks are provided to support, not hinder, instruction. Using software on the network is one means of delivering instruction. While a functional network is important, it has little meaning for teachers and students if they cannot use it appropriately. Take a realistic look at the amount of time required to install and troubleshoot software, then allocate resources accordingly. This may mean limiting the size of the network to something that is manageable, or augmenting existing technical support through student training or use of interns from local college, or other training programs.

## SOFTWARE STANDARDIZATION

A list of "acceptable" software is created and staff is informed that no other programs may be installed on the network. The rationale for this approach is twofold. First, by licensing certain programs for every workstation, the school or district receives a discount on bulk purchases. Second, technical support staff needs to learn a limited number of programs for troubleshooting.

**The reality**—Software standardization *does* result in savings on purchases and technical support. Initial training can also be standardized, leading to further savings. However, many educators resist standardization because they believe that this approach limits their ability to make decisions about instructional materials used in individual classrooms. Another objection is that standardization may squelch creativity and preclude researching and using new programs. Finally, standardization does not necessarily solve the problem of dealing with software upgrades.

**Antidote**—Recognize that standardization is a mixed blessing that requires staff buy-in. Make provisions to encourage educators to continue to seek out new, innovative uses of technology in classrooms. One solution is to establish a process for teachers to propose and implement small pilots of new software. Another possibility is to use standardization along with a software review committee whose charge includes finding and evaluating new products. Finally, in the case of staying current with upgrades, it may be more cost-efficient to lease software rather than purchase programs outright. Leasing can include provisions for automatic upgrades. This may also make it easier for the list of approved programs to maintain more fluidity.

Increasing numbers of teachers, administrators, and technical support staff are expressing concerns about methods used for selecting and installing software. As schools and districts continue to expand computer networks, the requirements for security and technical support will also grow. And in most instances, individual schools will be required to relinquish at least some local control to adhere to district policies and procedures designed to protect the entire network. Site administrators must take a leading role in the development of new policies and procedures to ensure that teachers and students have access to the technology they need in a timely fashion.

## ADDITIONAL RESOURCES

You can learn more by accessing these online resources:

enGauge, Robust Access–Anytime, Anywhere: Technology Resources (http://www.ncrel.org/engauge/framewk/acc/acchrub.htm): Although slightly dated, this continuum addresses many issues administrators need to consider when crafting standards for hardware and software. Note the emphasis on balance between instructional needs and tech support.

Lake Washington School District, Standards (www.lkwash.wednet .edu/lwsd/html/programs/technology/standards/): An example of a K–12 district standardization policy.

"Setting the Standard," at Technology Leader's Toolkit: http://www .thesnorkel.org/toolkit/articles/Standards.pdf (n.d.). Reading about establishing standards for hardware and software from the perspective of a technology coordinator.

"What Can Be Done About Tech Support?" at edtechnot.com: http:// www.edtechnot.com/notarticle502.html (n.d.). Another tech coordinator weighs in on why standardization is important.

Sonoma State University Information Technology, Why Hardware & Software Standards? (http://www.sonoma.edu/it/support/reason .html): Use this site, which explains the university's standardization policy, as a sample. There is also a link to information about how to request to add something to the list of approved hardware/software.

## QUESTIONS FOR DISCUSSION

1. What are the major issues faced in your site/district related to network security and reliability?

2. Describe measures taken in your site/district to protect the network and equipment.

3. Does your site/district currently have a policy regarding standardization of hardware and software purchases? Why, or why not?

4. Would a software approval committee work well in your site/district? Explain.

5. What is your site/district policy regarding network administrator rights? Is this policy effective?

6. What provisions are made in your site/district to encourage use of new technologies? Explain.

7. Describe an ideal approach to balancing the need to protect the network and equipment with teachers' needs for flexible, ingenious instruction.

# 17

## *The Evolving Role of the Technology Coordinator*

Increasing numbers of administrators are recognizing that staffing a technology coordinator is a critical step toward protecting their investment in technology. And it's not just a matter of keeping the equipment up and running. Teacher support, data collection and analysis, parent education, and other tasks are being relegated to technology coordinators. Read on to learn more about how this position is expanding in breadth and importance.

Fifteen years ago there was a school of thought that said that exemplary technology coordinators would work themselves out of a job within the foreseeable future. Those who espoused this theory believed that once schools had computers in place and teachers had mastered the basics, technology use would take off under its own steam and transform classroom education. However, with major changes in the field of technology occurring about every six months, we can see that, rather than becoming extinct, the role of the technology coordinator has expanded in scope and importance both for school districts and individual sites.

---

SOURCE: *Today's School*, January/February 2004

Many schools still struggle with who and what a technology coordinator should be. This position has been difficult for schools and districts to define from the start. The focus on buying "stuff," a lack of understanding of total cost of ownership (TCO) factors, and the assumption that teachers would be able to figure out instructional technology on their own have contributed to the confusion. Today's technology coordinators run the gamut from classified or certificated employees to administrators who range from volunteers to full-time staff. What may have started out as a person who did basic troubleshooting and handholding has evolved into something quite different. Most technology coordinators are now responsible for taking care of the hardware and software from installation and troubleshooting through repair and maintenance, including not only networks but also telephone systems and other equipment. In addition, coordinators take a lead role in technology planning, professional development, grant writing, equipment procurement, budgeting, and anything else related to technology use, up to and including providing direct instruction to students. They often have additional, non-technology assignments as well. With the reporting requirements for No Child Left Behind (NCLB) and other funding sources, many technology coordinators are also taking responsibility for data collection and analysis (Quality Education Data, Inc., forecasts that schools will spend an additional $60 million on technology in 2003–04 to meet NCLB requirements).

This is a huge job. But if statistics can be believed, most schools and districts are not allocating adequate resources for this position. Survey results reported by the U.S. Department of Education's National Center for Education Statistics in 2000 and analyzed by *Education Week* for its *Technology Counts 2003* report showed that just 16 percent of U.S. schools and only 17 percent of reporting districts had a full-time technology coordinator on staff. A variety of strategies were in place to fill the gap, including using full-time teachers who also had the title technology coordinator (21 percent); using library/media specialists in this role (14 percent); and other, less-formal arrangements (25 percent). Seven percent of the schools and districts had no technology coordinator at all. This scattered approach to technology support flies in the face of what we have learned about successful technology implementation, where experience has shown that a reliable infrastructure and ongoing teacher training and support are critical.

Site-based managed public schools may not be able to depend upon the district to provide the level of support required. Independent and private schools are definitely on their own. So what level of staffing do these schools need to provide adequate support? Timothy Landeck, director of technology services in Alisal Union School District in Salinas, California, and cochair of the Technology Coordinators Special Interest Group for Computer Using Educators (CUE), suggests that elementary schools need at least one part-time technician to handle infrastructure issues and one part-time person to deal with instruction and with data collection and analysis. He recommends that middle and high schools staff at least one full-time person in each of these areas to provide adequate support. Let's take a closer look at these recommendations and some strategies that can help you achieve this level of staffing.

## SUPPORTING THE INFRASTRUCTURE

You must get a handle on the current state of your school's infrastructure and the maintenance demands that will be placed on a technology coordinator. Chances are that in middle and high schools you'll discover that this is a full-time job in itself. Landeck cautions that in situations where a full-time technology coordinator is expected to divide time between infrastructure maintenance and instructional support, she or he nearly always finds that the majority of time is spent doing troubleshooting and repair. Therefore, it may be more efficient to create two part-time positions where responsibilities are divided and clearly defined.

You may not be able to afford a fully trained technician, but you have alternatives. Consider recruiting for the position among computer science students at community colleges or universities. While you will have turnover, this is a good opportunity for students to have a paid internship experience and an affordable way for you to offer on-site support. You may be able to develop a partnership with a local college to provide unpaid internships for students to earn credits. Landeck supports the use of interns for another reason. He points out that technicians do not always understand the educational ramifications of decisions they make regarding equipment standardization, locking down desktops, and software selection, especially when these decisions make perfect sense from a maintenance standpoint. Landeck reports that technicians in Alisal who have gone through an internship program in a K–12 setting tend to be more sensitive to the unintended instructional consequences of decisions they make to protect the infrastructure.

Other options include outsourcing your infrastructure support by purchasing extended warranties or negotiating technical support in the purchase or lease price for equipment. Middle and high schools also frequently use their own students for infrastructure support.

## SUPPORTING INSTRUCTION

Teachers need ongoing support before they are willing to incorporate technology use in the classroom. *Lessons Learned: Factors Influencing the Effective Use of Technology for Teaching and Learning* (www.seirtec.org/publications/lessons.pdf), published by SEIR♦TEC, reports that workshops alone aren't enough. In order to provide the ongoing support teachers need to shift to use of technology-infused instructional strategies, you must have an on-site technology coordinator who can focus on working with teaching staff. In elementary schools this can be a part-time person, perhaps a teacher whose assignment is one-half classroom time and one-half technology coordinator time. In larger middle and high schools, this person must be, if at all possible, full-time. Schools that receive federal funds can use some of this money to fund the technology coordinator. Virtually all NCLB funding allows for technology expenditures, including professional development.

## DATA COLLECTION AND ANALYSIS

Schools accepting NCLB funding and other grant funds are just beginning to understand the full impact of reporting requirements. The level of data collection and disaggregation expected cannot be accomplished without using technology support. Doug Prouty, technology specialist in the Contra Costa, California, County Office of Education and cochair of the Technology Coordinators Special Interest Group for CUE, reports that as school administrators make data collection and analysis a high priority he sees increasing numbers of districts and schools turning to their technology coordinators for assistance. "The biggest swing is a need to utilize data to support any implementation and to show that existing programs are standards-based and increase test scores. Technology coordinators are being asked to assist everyone who is trying to use data," says Prouty. Prouty also believes that the challenge lies in the fact that most technology coordinators are not experts in data-driven decision making and most assessment specialists are not technology experts. "In order to make well-reasoned decisions about Student Information Systems and/or data warehousing, individuals who have worked in isolation in the past must now pull together if they are to be successful in meeting reporting requirements." Again, schools receiving federal funds can use some of these monies to pay for the cost of reporting. Schools using grant funds from other sources should include "hidden" data collection and analysis costs in their evaluation budgets.

Most schools have made large investments in equipment. It is important that they protect this investment and enable teachers and students to make good use of technology by providing adequate on-site support. If your school already provides support at or above the levels discussed here, you are to be commended. If your school's on-site support is lacking, make a plan to correct the situation. The job won't get smaller and the need won't diminish.

## ADDITIONAL RESOURCES

In addition to the resources cited above, you can learn more by accessing these online resources:

Kansas Technology Coordinators Network: www.ktcn.org/. Visit the survey area (www.ktcn.org/survey/survey.html) where you can review data going back to 1999 relative to the role of technology coordinators in Kansas.

"Working with Your Technology Coordinator" in *Teaching Today:* www .glencoe.com/sec/teachingtoday/educationupclose.phtml/53 (January 2005). This brief article offers tips for educators who work with technology coordinators.

The Snorkel: A Support Forum for K–12 Technology Leaders: http:// www.thesnorkel.org/. Current issues, tools, and how-to's for today's technology coordinators.

"The Successful Technology Coordinator," at techLEARNING: http:// www.techlearning.com/db_area/archives/WCE/archives/parham .htm (April 2001). This article lists the attributes of a successful tech- nology coordinator.

Technology Coordinator's Handbook: http://www.schools.pinellas .k12.fl.us/tchandbk/default.htm. Prepared by the Office of Instructional Technology, Pinellas, Florida, this site was created to provide support to school-based technology coordinators.

## QUESTIONS FOR DISCUSSION

1. Does your site/district staff currently include technology coor- dinators? Explain.

2. If your district has one or more technology coordinators, what are the responsibilities for this position? Are these respon- sibilities well aligned with the needs of your staff?

3. In your opinion, what should be the major responsibilities of a technology coordinator? Explain.

4. Assuming your site/district had the resources to hire the neces- sary staff, how would you recommend staffing for technology support?

5. Do you predict a growing or diminishing need for technology coordinators in the future? Explain.

6. In your current situation, who is currently responsible for site or districtwide data collection and analysis? Explain.

7. In your opinion, who should be responsible for school or districtwide data collection and analysis? Explain.

---

# 18

# *What to Do When Things Aren't Working*

It's not reasonable to expect teachers to regularly maintain and repair classroom hardware and software. However, the National Education Technology Standards for Teachers do state that teachers should have basic troubleshooting skills, and technicians often report that problems they're called in to fix could have been rectified had the teacher known a few simple troubleshooting tricks. Anytime classroom technology is down is lost instructional time. To save time and money, administrators and school leaders need to ensure that all staff members know and use a few troubleshooting strategies prior to calling for support.

*You boot up the computer you plan to use for a class presentation. Instead of the desktop, the following message appears on a black screen: "Non-system disk or disk error. Replace and strike any key when ready." Do you know what to do?*

*The computer is on and you can see the desktop, but when you try to open an application, nothing happens. Now what do you do?*

*A student has just finished a writing assignment. She prints her file, but the paper that comes out of the printer is blank. Can you correct the problem?*

---

SOURCE: *Today's Catholic Teacher*, August/September 2004

Technology that isn't working properly is a source of frustration for classroom teachers and students, particularly when on-site technical support isn't immediately available. As a teacher, you may have little or no control over the level of technical support provided by your school. However, in most instances you and your students can solve each of the problems described above in just a minute or two. Teachers and students need not be technical experts to take care of the majority of problems they encounter when using technology. All that's required is knowledge of a few simple troubleshooting strategies to try before giving up and waiting for a technician to arrive.

I asked two groups of technology coordinators and technicians to share troubleshooting tips for teachers and students that, based upon their experience, are the easiest and most effective for nontechies to try. Responses came from as far away as Australia and Hong Kong! As often happens when dealing with collective wisdom, 10 tips were suggested over and over again. I've compiled these into a list you can review and keep in your classroom for those times when something just isn't working. Teachers who feel confident in their own troubleshooting skills can use this list to instruct their students or classroom volunteers in basic troubleshooting. The strategies are grouped by four common types of problems. In addition to the tips and supporting information provided in this chapter, you may also access an abbreviated list of tips on my Web site at www.sjbrooks-young .com/id13.html. Click on the Troubleshooting Tips link. This file can be printed and made available to students and volunteers. Tips 3, 6, and 8 provide solutions for the situations described at the beginning of this chapter.

### The equipment will not power up:

**1. Check all cables and connections to be sure they are secure, and check the power strip to make sure it is turned on.** A loose connection or a switched off power strip can cause what appears to be a malfunction. Classrooms are busy places. Students stash backpacks under tables and accidentally kick cords when sitting down. These actions can loosen cables and cords enough to break a connection or flip a toggle switch on a power strip.

**2. Make sure that the computer and peripherals are turned on.** Classroom and lab computers are frequently on a master switch so users don't need to turn each device on and off separately. This works well until someone forgets and uses the switch on the piece of equipment to power down. Or teachers and students become distracted while booting up systems and forget to turn on the monitor or a peripheral. Look for a green light on each device that appears to be nonresponsive, and press the on/off switch if you don't see a light. This may seem painfully obvious, but many technicians report that when they arrive to make a repair all they need to do is turn on the power.

**You get an error message while booting up,
or software programs do not respond properly:**

**3. Check the disk drive(s).** A floppy disk left in a 3 ½– inch drive will cause the "Non-system disk or disk error" message to appear on the monitor screen. Remove the disk, press any key, and the computer should continue the start-up process.

**4. Close the program and reopen it.** On those occasions when a program is not responding properly, or appears to be frozen, save your work if possible, then close and reopen the program.

**5. Try running the program on a different computer.** This is especially helpful when you're using a browser to access the Internet but keep getting an error message. If you have the same problem on another computer, the problem is probably with the Internet connection rather than the software.

**6. Reboot the computer.** This suggestion was included by nearly every coordinator and technician who responded. If the computer is not working properly (e.g., you double-click on a program icon but the program does not open, or you've closed and reopened a program and it is still not responding), save your work if possible, then use the regular shut-down procedure. If the computer is frozen, try pressing the keys labeled Ctrl, Alt, and Del simultaneously on a PC, or using the Force Quit command on a Mac. If that doesn't work you may need to use the reset button or, in the worst-case scenario, unplug the computer in order to shut down. Then power up again. Ninety-nine percent of the time the computer will now work. Occasionally you may need to reboot more than once.

**The printer is on and connected, but is not printing properly:**

**7. Check the paper tray.** If you click on Print and nothing happens, check the paper tray to make sure it's loaded and closed completely. If there is paper and the tray is properly closed, try turning the printer off and on again. Sometimes the printer and the computer lose communication; this will reestablish the link between the two.

**8. Check the ink or toner cartridge.** If the printer is cranking out blank paper, check to see if the ink or toner cartridge is empty. For ink-jet printers, also check to make sure the plastic protection strip over the jets on the cartridge was removed before the cartridge was installed.

**The computer speakers are connected but you can't hear the sound:**

**9. Check the power switch.** Separate speakers often have their own on/off switch. Make sure they are powered on. If you're using a headset, make sure it's plugged in and is in the correct jack; often the headset jack is right next to a jack for a microphone.

**10. Turn up the volume.** Volume for many speakers can be controlled both by a knob on the speaker and by using a volume control feature through the computer's control panel. If you don't know how to adjust the volume using the computer, get directions from a technician before there's a problem.

## WHEN YOU NEED TO CALL FOR ASSISTANCE

There will be occasions when you need to ask for technical support. Keep your cool. Unless a piece of equipment has literally been shattered, chances are that it can be repaired. However, the technician will need some information in order to diagnose and fix what's wrong. Here are some things to do before you make that call:

1. An error message may appear on the screen; if so, write down exactly what it says.

2. Write down what was happening when the problem started. Be sure to include information about events that occurred that may have caused the problem (e.g., a power surge occurred, a new program was installed, a file was downloaded, or an accident happened, such as a liquid spill). Describe what you've done to try to solve the problem.

3. Identify when you could be available to meet with the technician to review the problem so you're prepared to make an appointment. The technician will be able to solve the problem more quickly after talking with you directly.

4. Use the proper protocol for reporting a problem. Several technicians stated that repairs are often delayed because teachers do not complete required paperwork or do not submit the request properly.

5. Place a note on the malfunctioning system or peripheral to alert other users. This is especially important when you're using shared equipment in a lab or library media center.

## PREVENTIVE MEASURES YOU CAN TAKE

Many of the problems that arise with classroom and lab computers could have been avoided. Establish some simple rules for classroom computer use, and follow them yourself! Here are suggestions for keeping your equipment up and running:

1. Do no install programs on your own. This includes downloading programs from the Internet.

2. Never open an e-mail attachment from someone you do not know.

3. Do not change the settings on computers.

4. Acquaint yourself with Help files by clicking on the Help command in the toolbar of any application you are using to find information about how to use the program.

5. Keep your computer's virus protection software up-to-date. If you're not sure how to do this, ask the technician for assistance before there's a problem.

6. Keep a log of previous problems and how they were solved. This can be a valuable resource for later reference.

7. Keep food and drinks away from equipment.

8. Actively monitor student use of computers.

As you increase your use of technology in the classroom, you also increase the odds that you will encounter problems. Knowing and using these troubleshooting tips will go a long way toward enabling you and your students to use technology independently. Your technician will also appreciate your efforts, knowing that when you call for support you really do need help.

## ADDITIONAL RESOURCES

In addition to the resources cited above, you can learn more by accessing these online resources:

Bali PC Advertiser, End of Year Tune-Up (PC): http://www.baliadver tiser.biz/articles/balipc/2005/end_year.html. A few simple steps teachers can take to leave their PCs in good shape for the fall. There are differences in various Windows operating systems. Be sure to read all the directions before beginning.

Cahokia School District #187, Computer Troubleshooting Help: http://www.cahokia.stclair.k12.il.us/Cptrblo.htm. A lengthy list of common problems and possible solutions.

Country Areas Program, New South Wales, Troubleshooting—Macintosh Computers: http://www.cap.nsw.edu.au/tech_help/trouble shooting.html. Several strategies for solving simple software problems on Macintosh computers.

International Society for Technology in Education, National Educational Technology Standards: http://www.iste.org/Template.cfm?Section= NETS&Template=/TaggedPage/TaggedPageDisplay.cfm&TPLID=17 &ContentID=824. Links to standards for students, teachers, and administrators. Visit each section to review references to troubleshooting skills for that particular role.

University of Wisconsin–River Falls, Computer Maintenance Tutorial: http://www.uwrf.edu/ccs/training/maintain.htm. Four routine maintenance steps for better computer performance. Note: As written, the final step works for Windows 95, 98, and ME. For Windows 2000, NT, and XP, use Chkdsk.

## QUESTIONS FOR DISCUSSION

1. Describe the most common technical glitches that result in downtime for technology at your site.

2. Explain current troubleshooting policies and procedures in place in your district or school.

3. Describe the teacher's current role in basic troubleshooting at your site/district.

4. What are the benefits and drawbacks in the current policies and procedures for troubleshooting?

5. How could these policies and procedures be improved?

6. Do you think that teachers should be required to complete a basic troubleshooting course? Why, or why not?

7. Explain your thoughts about asking students to provide basic troubleshooting services for teachers and staff.

# PART IV

## *Legal and Social Concerns*

Security, online safety, equal access for students with a variety of disabilities, and misuse of technology are just a few of the concerns administrators must deal with as technology use increases. The chapters in this section address common issues that administrators must anticipate and resolve.

# 19

## *Teachers, Students, and Technology Use*

### *Some Cautions*

Increasing numbers of classrooms are going online. This means that both adults and students are more likely to experience a virtual mishap, or even to intentionally engage in online misbehavior. Wise administrators anticipate these eventualities and have a plan for how to deal with them fairly and reasonably. This chapter identifies issues and offers resources administrators can use to help faculty and students make appropriate use of the Web.

As technology use in classrooms increases, so do questions concerning the rights and responsibilities of adult and student users. Teachers must navigate this ever-changing landscape, anticipating situations that may arise and finding solutions to challenges that did not exist until recently. While it is mandated that schools that receive E-Rate or Elementary and Secondary Education Act (ESEA) funds use the requirements of the Children's Internet Protection Act (CIPA) to plan for legal questions they

SOURCE: *Today's Catholic Teacher*, March 2002

may face, the requirements provide a useful guideline for all schools. In addition to the familiar issue of filtering Internet access to protect students from inappropriate Web content, CIPA requires expanded Internet safety policies and dissemination of information about policies.

Internet safety policies deal with issues beyond filtering, including e-mail, chat rooms, hacking, release of personal information, and measures taken beyond filtering to protect students from inappropriate material; these are all concerns that may be dealt with through comprehensive acceptable use policies (AUPs). CIPA also allows for differentiation between student and adult use. While some of the provisions may not be practical to implement, it spotlights the fact that it is wise for schools to have a separate AUP for adults.

Finally, CIPA requires that a public meeting be held to explain the policies for filtering and Internet safety. This is important whether or not the school falls under the oversight of CIPA because, in order to enforce an AUP, a district must be able to prove that parents and students had ample opportunity to learn about its provisions.

## STUDENT USE OF TECHNOLOGY

A current AUP needs to be in place even when students don't have Internet access, because a well-written AUP covers all aspects of student use of school-owned equipment. For the most effective implementation, this policy must be reviewed and updated annually, signed yearly by students and parents, and enforced consistently. It is important for teachers to clearly understand the terms of the school's student AUP, to discuss them with students, and to model following the guidelines. For example, some schools decide not to provide e-mail addresses to students. There have been instances where teachers circumvent the AUP by setting up free student e-mail accounts through another source. However, when students see adults ignoring policy, they will infer that they can, too. If e-mail accounts are offered and the AUP states that they will be monitored, the network administrator needs to spot-check accounts occasionally so students understand there is follow-through. Ongoing enforcement of the AUP makes it more likely that serious consequences can be administered if needed: sloppy enforcement makes this unlikely.

Teachers need to actively supervise students using the Internet for their own protection as well as for students'. In two recent cases in Florida, teachers were arrested when it was discovered that pornography sites were being accessed from their classroom computers. Charges were dropped after it was demonstrated that students were responsible, but new policies at the schools state clearly that teachers must do all they can to prevent this kind of incident through instruction and supervision.

Despite incidents like those mentioned above, students' misuse of technology is often accidental. The best filtering software still occasionally allows access to inappropriate sites. Although you cannot protect students from every inappropriate Web site, you can teach them to structure Internet searches and use clues to help identify sites that are suspect prior to entering them. A resource for older students and adults explaining how to effectively search the Internet may be found at Learn the Net .com: Searching the Web (www.learnthenet.com/english/html/31wsearc .htm). This brief tutorial explains how search engines work. Searching the Internet: Recommended Sites and Search Techniques (http://library .albany.edu/internet/search.html) from the University at Albany Libraries' site is another good tool.

Also teach students to scrutinize their search results by reading the brief descriptions provided and to look carefully at the URL for each site prior to going there. Although not foolproof, sites sponsored by educational institutions, governmental agencies, and reputable organizations are usually appropriate for students, and the Web addresses will end in ".edu," ".gov," or ".org." Students who understand how to read a URL will know that the official government-sponsored White House Web site address would not end in ".com."

With increased use of multimedia presentations and student-created Web pages, copyright infringement is a growing concern. Schools need to have a clearly defined copyright policy that is explained to students and parents, with reminders frequently embedded in lessons. Because it is so easy to copy or download software or text, image, and sound files, students have difficulty understanding that they may be breaking the law when they do this. Plagiarism is also a problem. Students who purchase or download entire term papers know they are cheating, but students who copy a paragraph here or there and change the wording a bit may not understand why they are guilty of cheating as well. Instruction in information literacy that teaches children how to use information to create work they can legitimately call their own helps clarify this concept for students.

## ADULT USE OF TECHNOLOGY

Adult use of school-provided technology needs to be regulated through a separate AUP for staff. Again, this policy should be reviewed and updated annually, and then signed by every employee each school year. Teachers need to understand the provisions of the AUP to avoid inadvertent abuse of school resources.

Most often, employee misuse is unintentional. For example, while students are working in the lab, the teacher decides to take a peek at personal e-mail and to make a quick personal purchase on eBay. Or a teacher uses a school computer to write a letter for a part-time business she or he operates from home. While these actions aren't necessarily illegal, they may be considered misuses of time and equipment, and can result in disciplinary action. Schools need to have well-defined guidelines for personal use of equipment.

What does a teacher need to know about using school equipment and electronic communication? This should be spelled out clearly in the AUP, but here are some basics. E-mail written on school-owned equipment or sent via a school e-mail account is not private. The school administration has the right to monitor the volume of e-mail you send and to read its contents. Employees have faced disciplinary actions due to excessive personal use of e-mail during the workday as well as questionable content of e-mail.

If your school falls under regulations for maintaining paper correspondence files for defined periods of time, electronic correspondence also falls under this regulation. This means that if you are required to keep files of paper student progress reports or notes to parents about student progress or behavior, you must also keep electronic communication about these topics for the same period of time. In the past, some schools have maintained that messages of this type are regularly erased due to hard drive storage constraints, but a recent court decision states that lack of storage is not an acceptable reason for deleting this kind of correspondence.

While adults have more latitude than students when exploring the Internet, they are also legally restricted from accessing obscene or pornographic sites when using school equipment or accounts. Schools have the right to monitor the Internet sites that teachers visit while using the school's equipment or Internet service provided by the school. A school employee might be visiting inappropriate sites after the workday, but even if the trail is left after hours, there can be serious consequences. Over the last two years several district superintendents of public schools have resigned or been dismissed because their computer hard drives contained evidence that the equipment had been used for inappropriate purposes during and after school hours.

## SCHOOL WEB SITES

Many schools host Web sites hoping to increase home/school communication. Teachers are often asked to post class information including homework assignments, examples of student work, and recaps of recent activities. If your school maintains a Web site there are issues concerning student privacy that must be addressed. For example, the school needs to have a policy in place regarding what can be posted and procedures for obtaining written parent permission prior to posting photographs or work. Even with written permission, consider keeping students' names private, or using first names only. Some schools opt to use photos that are slightly out of focus. Parents have raised objections to having any information about their children posted, and this desire for privacy must be respected.

## CONCLUSION

Questions concerning the rights and responsibilities of school technology users will continue to arise. Individual schools will benefit from working with their diocesan or district offices to ensure that their AUPs are up-to-date and to develop Internet safety policies as part of the AUP or as separate documents. Teachers who know and conform to these policies will be able to engage in high quality technology experiences both personally and with their students.

## ADDITIONAL RESOURCES

In addition to the resources cited above, you can learn more by accessing these online resources:

> Center for Safe and Responsible Internet Use, Safe and Responsible Use of the Internet: http://csriu.org/onlinedocs/pdf/srui/sruilisting .html. A downloadable guide written specifically for educators.

> Federal Communications Commission: Children's Internet Protection Act (http://www.fcc.gov/cgb/consumerfacts/cipa.html). Background information on CIPA.

> "How to Create a Bad Acceptable Use Policy Document (and Have It Survive)!" in *The teachers.net Gazette*, Vol. 3, No. 3: http://www .teachers.net/gazette/MAR02/reilly.html (March 2002). Important issues to consider when crafting and Acceptable Use Policy.

> Virginia Department of Education Division of Technology, Acceptable Use Policies—A Handbook: http://www.pen.k12.va.us/go/VDOE/ Technology/AUP/home.shtml. Updated to include CIPA requirements.

---

## QUESTIONS FOR DISCUSSION

1. Describe the provisions of your site/district AUPs for students and adults.

2. Explain your role in implementation and monitoring of AUPs.

3. Explain how parents are kept informed about the student AUP.

4. Based upon your reading, are your existing site/district AUPs compliant with CIPA requirements? Explain.

5. What are your site/district policies regarding personal use of the Internet at school for students? For teachers and staff?

6. What are the strengths and weaknesses of your current site/district AUPs?

7. How could you improve or enhance implementation of AUPs at your site/district?

# 20

## *Copyright and Technology Use in the Classroom*

> Growing use of the Internet and other technology-based tools brings up many serious legal questions for educators. Proactive schools/districts position themselves to deal with these concerns through the use of acceptable use and copyright policies. How well informed are you and your staff, when it comes to fair use and other copyright information?

When filmstrip projectors and ditto machines were high-end technologies, there wasn't much concern about copyright infringement in the classroom. With today's advances in technology, downloading, replicating, and redistributing all sorts of copyrighted materials is a piece of cake. In fact, it's become so easy that many teachers and students don't realize that they may be doing something illegal. The posting of student work, performances, and other activities on the Internet strips away classroom walls and invites closer scrutiny of how and when

SOURCE: *Today's Catholic Teacher,* April 2003

copyrighted materials are used in teaching. The conversation has moved beyond what's being posted on school or classroom Web sites to what software is available on school systems, how video is obtained and used in classrooms, and more.

How current is your knowledge of copyright law for the use of various technologies including video, software, the Internet, and copy machines to share information and materials with students? Let's begin with a pop quiz to see if you recognize some of the elements of copyright law that affect classrooms.

The following scenarios describe events that commonly occur in schools. In each case, ask yourself: Is this action permissible under copyright law?

1. As a reward for the first-grade classes' victory in a reading competition, you pop gallons of popcorn and invite the students to the cafeteria to view the Don Bluth film *An American Tail*, rented from a local video store.

2. A junior-high science teacher purchases a class license to install a software program on 30 workstations. There are 30 students, and each uses an individual station during the class period. When a 31st student is enrolled, the teacher loads the program on another computer for this student to use during class.

3. Fifth-grade students download images from the Internet to use in multimedia projects for the classroom. Some of the images are copyrighted, and students do not take the time to obtain permission for classroom use.

4. A teacher purchases one copy of a workbook that supplements a classroom text, and then duplicates the exercises for student use.

5. A high school student uses brief (less than 30 seconds each) copyrighted music clips to enhance a social science multimedia project.

## COPYRIGHT AND FAIR USE

Before moving on to the answers and explanations for the quiz questions, here's a quick overview of the purpose of copyright and the idea of fair use, which will provide some insight into the reasoning behind the answers.

Title 17 Section 102 (a) of the United States Code states that any original work in some tangible form that can be perceived and/or reproduced may be copyrighted. Some examples include: written work, such as books, essays, plays, and articles; music and lyrics; art work including pictures, graphics, and sculpture; movies and other visual recordings; and sound recordings. Although the code was recently extended, there is a time limit on copyright protection. Once a work is no longer protected by copyright, it becomes part of the public domain and may be reproduced and used without permission.

In the meantime, to provide public access to copyrighted material, the concept of *fair use* was formalized in the Copyright Act of 1976. Educators are permitted to copy and use materials in their classrooms for instructional purposes within certain limitations. Fair use is not free rein. The law includes four standards to use when determining fair use, but it's left to the individual to make case-by-case decisions. There are no cut-and-dried answers; however, here are four questions teachers can ask themselves to help determine what is fair use:

1. Is your planned use of the material noncommercial and instructional?

   Your answer should be yes to both.

2. What is the nature of the material (i.e., nonfiction or fiction, published or unpublished)?

   Use of published nonfiction more often falls under fair use than use of unpublished or fictional material because it's factual information that's readily available to the public.

3. How much of the original work do you intend to use?

   Excerpts are usually permissible, but there are limits.

4. Does your use of the work negatively affect the copyright owner's ability to earn profits from the work?

   Your answer should be no.

Since the last major revision of the Copyright Act in 1976, technology has advanced at an extraordinary rate. Two recent acts, the Digital Millennium Copyright Act (1998) and the Technology, Education, and Copyright Harmonization Act (2002), each address issues raised with digital technology and in distance learning environments. Guidelines have been developed to assist educators, librarians, and others in determining fair use, but there is still room for interpretation.

## ANSWERS TO THE QUIZ

Armed with this short explanation of copyright and fair use, let's return to the quiz questions.

1. No, it is not permissible to rent and show a movie as a reward, in a classroom or anywhere else on campus. It is legal to rent and show movies in a classroom when there is an instructional purpose. If you wish to show a movie for entertainment or as a reward, you need to contact the production company and pay an entertainment fee.

2. No, this is not permissible. Although the science teacher has purchased a class license for the software program, the license limits

simultaneous use to 30 workstations. Using the program on an additional workstation violates this agreement. It is legal in some circumstances to install software on more systems, but the school is then required to monitor use to limit it to the number of stations covered in the license at any given time.

3. Yes, this is an example of fair use. Students may download and use copyrighted images from the Internet for a classroom project as long as the projects are not distributed outside the classroom. The teacher would cross the line if, for example, she decided to post the projects on the World Wide Web.

4. No, this is not permissible. Consumable workbooks are published with the intent that they will be purchased for, and used by, one student. By making copies of the worksheets, the teacher is impacting the copyright owner's ability to profit from the work.

5. Yes, this is an example of fair use. Students may use very short audio clips (the fair use guidelines for educational multimedia limit these clips to 30 seconds each) as part of a multimedia project. Again, the project should not be posted on the World Wide Web.

## COPYRIGHT POLICIES

So how is a teacher supposed to know what is permissible? This is where a copyright policy becomes an essential tool. Because of the complexities and changing interpretations of copyright law, a well-developed policy can guide administrators, teachers, staff, and students in making educated decisions about their use of copyrighted materials in teaching and learning. Well-balanced copyright policies not only explain what educators should not do, they also serve as a guide for what they may do. It would be a shame to restrict teacher and student access to valuable resources out of the fear of doing something wrong.

In a public school system, the district office typically takes responsibility for developing a copyright policy. In Catholic schools, each individual school may need to assume this task, although it would be worthwhile to contact the diocesan education office for guidance. Copyright policies today must include guidelines for a wide range of topics including photocopying, performances, music, taping television broadcasts, use of the Internet, computer software, multimedia, distance learning, and the school library's role in duplicating materials and electronic subscriptions. It's also important to provide basic information about copyright and fair use.

A number of resources are available for model copyright policies and other information. Groton Public Schools in Mystic, Connecticut, hosts a Web page that includes the district's copyright policy, which is held up as a model for other schools and districts. It can be accessed at http://groton.k12.ct.us/docs/policies/cimanual.pdf. The Wisconsin Department of Public Education hosts a site called Copyright Resources for Schools and Libraries at http://dpi.wi.gov/lbstat/copyres.html.The University of Texas at Austin offers the online Crash Course in Copyright at www.utsystem.edu/ogc/IntellectualProperty/cprtindx.htm#top.

But a copyright policy is only as good as its enforcement. Staff, students, and parents must be educated about the policy and its provisions. Along with staff in-services and direct student instruction about copyright, some schools include an abbreviated form of the copyright policy in the AUP that is distributed and signed annually. Reference charts that outline the basics should be available in the library, classrooms, and work areas where materials are duplicated as well as in staff and student handbooks. WestEd provides a sample copyright notice for this purpose at www.wested.org/techplan/copyright/welcome.html.

You may think this is overkill. After all, are there copyright police keeping classrooms under surveillance? While it's true that most violations go unnoticed, the technologies that make it easier to break the law also enable closer monitoring of some types of infractions. Companies in the software and entertainment industries as well as organizations like the Business Software Alliance have recently launched a number of investigations into schools' use or misuse of their products. Some of these investigations have resulted in large monetary judgments against the schools involved.

But even more important than the risk of getting caught is the fact that intentional copyright infringement is wrong. When educators decide to make that unauthorized copy of a software program or duplicate multiple chapters from books, they are, by their actions, telling students this behavior is okay. On the other hand, when a school staff establishes, implements, and adheres to a formal copyright policy, teachers model appropriate behavior and can help students make good decisions about fair use of copyrighted materials in their own use of technology. We all benefit from working and learning in an environment that supports informed, ethical decision making.

## ADDITIONAL RESOURCES

In addition to the resources cited above, you can learn more by accessing these online resources:

> Adventures of Cyberbee, Copyright with Cyberbee: http://www.cyberbee.com/copyrt.html. Overview of copyright issues, links to online resources, and a copyright lesson plan.

> Future of Networking Technologies for Learning, Copyright and K–12: Who Pays in the Network Era?: http://www.ed.gov/Technology/Futures/rothman.html. This archived article offers extensive discussion

about copyright and schools. Topics include: K–12, Networks, and Copyright Today; The Law–The Present and the Proposed; Attitudes of Educators and Others Toward Copyright Law; and Options.

Keystone Central School District, Fair Use of Copyright in the K–12 Classroom: http://www.kcsd.k12.pa.us/technology/copyright/index.html. This site includes slide shows, case studies, and teacher tips.

TechLearning, Copyright Guidelines for Administrators: http://www.techlearning.com/copyrightguide/;jsessionid=MHY2ILRELXMQGQSNDBGCKH0CJUMEKJVN. Two pdf files are available here. One is a primer on copyright and the other is a chart of guidelines.

U.S. Copyright Office, Copyright: http://www.copyright.gov/. The official site of the U.S. Copyright Office.

## QUESTIONS FOR DISCUSSION

1. How well did you do on the quiz?

2. Which answers did you know, and which answers did you miss? Explain.

3. How does your site/district address copyright with staff?

4. How does your site/district address copyright with students?

5. In your opinion, are your site/district copyright practices adequate? Explain.

6. Many educators believe that copyright law should not apply to them. What are your thoughts about this?

7. How has this chapter changed your thinking about K–12 education and copyright law? Explain.

---

# 21

# *Monitoring Student Internet Use*

## *It's More Than Filtering*

Since the E-Rate was established in 1996, the number of schools in the United States that have Internet connectivity in classrooms and labs has skyrocketed. Safety and ethics are two critical issues for teachers whose students use the Internet. However, many teachers aren't certain how to address these hot topics and their administrators aren't sure either! This chapter gives an overview of steps educators can take to effectively monitor student use of the Internet.

With all the hoopla surrounding the Children's Internet Protection Act (CIPA) requirement that schools and libraries block access to certain types of Internet sites, it's easy to forget that a protected environment is just one piece of the monitoring puzzle. Comprehensive monitoring also requires that teachers know what activities students engage in

---

SOURCE: *Today's Catholic Teacher*, November/December 2003

while online, even when objectionable sites are blocked. For example, CIPA monitoring requirements mandate that schools

- Provide for the safety of students using e-mail and chat rooms or other methods of electronic communication, such as instant messaging
- Have policies and procedures in place that deal with the provision of personal information about students
- Develop procedures for dealing with students who unlawfully hack into computer systems

In addition, although copyright is not addressed in CIPA, schools are also increasingly held accountable for students' violations of copyright law. While blocking technology may be part of the answer, it is certainly not sufficient to meet all the requirements listed above.

To successfully implement a comprehensive plan for monitoring students' Internet use, parents, administrators, and teachers all must be on the same page. This chapter explores the three basic areas that constitute comprehensive monitoring of student Internet use: creating a protected online environment; defining the parameters of acceptable use; and, most importantly, proactive supervision of students as they use the Internet.

## CREATING A PROTECTED ONLINE ENVIRONMENT

Internet filters are products that are used to control access to Web sites and electronic communication. Due to the sheer number of Web sites, filters tend to rely on mechanical methods for identifying objectionable materials, using keywords and phrases to block access. Determining the value of many sites is very subjective, so even in cases where a human makes the final decision the results may be uneven. Most filtering products can be customized to a degree, allowing a network administrator to identify filtering levels for students and adults or to modify the list of blocked sites.

Problems arise when parents and educators misunderstand the capabilities of the filter being used and assume that once a filter is in place, students will not be able to access objectionable materials. Unfortunately, filters are not infallible, and students will, from time to time, access an inappropriate site. Another issue is overfiltering. This occurs when, due to the mechanical nature of filtering, students cannot access legitimate sites for research or classroom activities.

To avoid misconceptions about filtering products, parents and teachers must take part in the selection of the product to be used. It's also a good idea to hold informational meetings to explain the filter and its capabilities to those adults who are not involved in its selection. Teachers must also know what to do when an unacceptable site is not blocked or when students are not able to access legitimate sites.

## ACCEPTABLE USE POLICIES (AUPs)

AUPs are the natural vehicle for addressing issues such as student hacking, access to personal information, copyright, and electronic communication (i.e., e-mail, chat rooms, or instant messaging). A signed AUP should be required for any student or staff member who accesses the Internet using school equipment or a school-provided Internet service provider, and it should be renewed annually. Parent signatures should be required for any student under age 18. To effectively implement an AUP, the school administrator must have the support of parents and teachers. It's important to include representatives from each of these groups in the development and updating of this document, which should also be reviewed by an attorney to ensure that its provisions are legally enforceable.

Once the AUP is developed, informational meetings for parents and teachers are critical; the adults must have a clear understanding of what the policies entail and how they will be enforced. Administrators who neglect this step often encounter problems when teachers don't enforce AUP rules uniformly or when parents claim they didn't understand the full impact of the document they signed.

## PROACTIVE SUPERVISION

No matter how much care is given to selecting a filtering product or how comprehensive an AUP may be, they're only as good as the ongoing supervision in classrooms and labs. Teachers and support staff must know their responsibilities and take a proactive role in the day-to-day implementation of monitoring procedures. Here are 10 tips for teachers following up in this all-important area:

**1. Know and follow the provisions of the acceptable use policy.** Well-written AUPs clearly define the teacher's responsibilities for monitoring student use of the Internet; a wise teacher is informed about the AUP requirements and then follows through. Failure to do so may mean that students who intentionally abuse their access to the Internet cannot be held accountable for the misuse.

**2. Model acceptable use and adherence to copyright policies.** Students pay attention to the behavior of adults around them. Teachers must practice what they preach, setting a good example for the students in their care.

**3. Teach specific lessons about Internet safety skills, and clarify the AUP and copyright policy for students.** Do not assume that students understand all the provisions of the AUP. Regularly reinforce the rules through instruction that will help students become responsible Internet users. Teachers who are not sure how to develop Internet safety lessons can find examples on the Web. The SafeKids.com site at www.safekids .com or Cyber Smart! at www.cybersmart.org/home offer ideas and tools teachers can use with students.

**4. Provide opportunities for students to find solutions for handling uncomfortable situations online.** Fire drills are scheduled so students know what to do in an actual emergency. The goal of Internet safety lessons is for students to have safe Internet experiences no matter where they are. The protected environment at school may prevent unhappy incidents there, but what happens when students are at home or in another situation where Internet access is not so well protected? Develop scenarios and ask students to discuss how they would handle various potentially bad situations. The Teen area of NetSmartz (www.netsmartz.org) includes several scenarios appropriate for discussion with students in middle grades through high school.

**5. Arrange computers and peripherals for easy monitoring.** Circular hubs of computers or centers set off in a corner are very difficult for teachers to monitor. When arranging computers in a classroom or lab ask, "How can these systems be placed to support learning and also provide for ease of monitoring?" Think about printer location as well. In a classroom, place the printer next to the teacher's desk. In a lab, place the printer by the teaching station or, if one is available, in an adjoining lab office. A simple check on what students are printing can be very effective in cutting down on questionable use.

**6. Use a Web site evaluation tool when selecting sites for classroom use.** Sites that appear to be acceptable at first glance may not hold up under closer scrutiny. Some schools use a matrix or rubric for evaluating Web sites, but for those that do not, a number are available online. Visit the Assessment and Rubric Information area of Kathy Schrock's Web site at http://school.discovery.com/schrockguide/assess.html for links to a variety of evaluation tools.

**7. Complete all online activities yourself before using them with students.** Due to the changing nature of the Internet, teachers should review online material prior to using it with students. The importance of this type of review was recently underscored by an incident involving a highly reputable language arts site which offers literature-based online lesson plans, including links to outside sources. A teacher who had successfully used one of the lesson plans previously decided to use it with a new class. However, she didn't think to recheck the links before going online with her students. Unbeknownst to both the teacher and the site's webmaster, a linked Internet address had been acquired by a different company, and the third graders found themselves at a very inappropriate Web site. Yes, the language arts site should have had provisions for checking links; however, had the teacher checked the links herself, she would have avoided an unpleasant incident.

**8. Use online planning tools to create Internet-based lessons.** Teachers can ensure high quality online experiences for their students by using their own Internet-based lessons. There are free online lesson-planning tools are available to teachers, such as Filamentality (www.filamentality.com) and TrackStar (http://trackstar.hprtec.org/). The virtue of this approach to Internet-based activities is that teachers are in effect monitoring use by selecting just those sites that are high quality and relate directly to the curriculum. This also helps avoid wasting student time in unproductive searches and in accessing poor quality materials.

**9. Set up dummy e-mail addresses for sites that require registration.** From time to time, a really good Web site will ask users to log in using an e-mail address before they can access information on the site. If, in a teacher's opinion, the information on a site requiring this type of registration is worthwhile, the teacher can preregister using dummy e-mail accounts set up through the school's system or by using a free e-mail service such as Hotmail or Yahoo! (check to find out about school rules related to e-mail accounts first). When students need to access the site, they can simply type in an e-mail address that has been created for that purpose (i.e., student1@hotmail.com).

**10. Be visible.** Teachers need to monitor students while they are online by circulating around the room. Keeping an eye on computer monitors helps ensure that students are visiting appropriate sites, engaged in acceptable electronic communication, and observing copyright law.

Many educators have voiced concern that monitoring requirements seem to focus almost exclusively on the negative aspects of Internet use. While it's true that bad things can happen, it's also true that the Internet is a wonderful resource for students and teachers, providing access to materials that just wouldn't be available otherwise in classrooms. A proactive, balanced approach to monitoring student Internet use takes work, but the benefits to students and teachers are worth the effort.

## ADDITIONAL RESOURCES

In addition to the resources cited above, you can learn more by accessing these online resources:

4Kids.org, Safe Surfing: http://www.4kids.org/safesurf/. Students can learn safe surfing tips and adults are able to access resources about Internet safety, related laws, and more.

Consortium for School Networking, Cyber Security for the Digital District: http://www.securedistrict.org/. This site is designed specifically for school administrators and other leaders who must deal with Internet safety issues. Tools and information are available.

Information Technology Services, Computer Ethics Institute: http://www.brook.edu/ITS/CEI/CEI_HP.HTM. Access to articles about ethical use of the Internet, including the Ten Commandments of Computer Ethics.

Business Software Alliance, Play It Cyber Safe: http://www.playitcybersafe.com/. Students, parents, and teachers learn about safe, responsible use of the Internet through resources available on this site.

Disney Online, Surf Swell Island: http://www.disney.go.com/surfswell/index.html. Appropriate for grades K–6, this Disney site offers online activities for students as well as guides for parents and teachers.

## QUESTIONS FOR DISCUSSION

1. What steps are taken at your site/district to create a protected online environment for students and staff?

2. How is your site's/district's AUP implemented and enforced?

3. Give an example of how you encourage adults at your site/district to practice proactive supervision of students using the Internet.

4. Of the 10 steps for proactive supervision, which two are most critical in your opinion? Explain.

5. Of the 10 steps for proactive supervision, which two are least critical in your opinion? Explain.

6. How could your site/district increase its effectiveness in promoting safe and ethical use of the Internet?

7. How could you increase your own effectiveness in promoting safe and ethical use of the Internet?

# 22

# Spreading the Word Quickly

## Technology–Based Home/School Communication

Effective home/school communication is the bedrock for strong parental support of schools and involvement in programs. Many schools and districts are now using online communication along with more traditional approaches to keep parents informed: listservs, automated telephone messaging systems, homework hotlines, Web sites , and blogs are just a few of the strategies being used. These forms of communication are useful for both day-to-day notices and during emergencies, when school staff must get accurate information out to parents quickly.

When Hillside Middle School in Simi Valley, California, had to close in fall 2003 due to fires raging through the area, Principal Steve Pietrolungo was able to keep more than 700 parents informed about fire-related events through an e-mail list developed for the school's online newsletter. During the aftermath of Hurricane Isabel, parents of students at Trinity Episcopal School in Richmond, Virginia, were able to access

SOURCE: *Today's Catholic Teacher,* April 2004

information about school closings and reopenings through notices posted on the school's Web site in addition to information about television and radio stations that were broadcasting closure updates. Shortly after the school installed an automated message system, a bomb threat was called into the office at Cantwell Sacred Heart of Mary High School in Montebello, California. Principal David Chambers notified the authorities and took steps to ensure that students were safe. He then drafted and sent a message to all parents via the school's automated dialing system. Within minutes parents knew the facts about the bomb threat and were reassured that their children were safe and that the situation was being handled.

No matter how proactive educators may be, there will always be times during the year when unforeseen events make it imperative that parents be notified about an episode on campus, an emergency school closure, or some other incident. Printed notices take time to generate and often are buried in backpacks or tossed into wastebaskets. Many schools are turning to automating calling system—once used primarily for checking on absent students and setting up Homework Hotlines—and e-mail listservs when they need to get accurate information to parents quickly.

## COMMUNICATION TOOLS

A variety of solutions are available to educators who want to use e-mail or telephone systems to communicate important information to parents. If a large enough percentage of the school's parents have e-mail access that it's practical to rely on a listserv as a means of communication, it's usually possible to establish parent and staff e-mail lists using the existing e-mail system. However, in many instances more families have telephones than Internet access, leading schools to use automated dialing systems with e-mail as a secondary communication method. Here are three popular telephone-based systems:

**Notification Technologies' (formerly PACE, Partnership for Academic and Community Excellence) Connect-ED:** www.notification.com. Connect-ED uses the existing telephone system and Internet access to allow school administrators to record, send, and track telephone messages. Users log onto the secure Web site, record a message over the telephone, identify message recipients (e.g., staff members, parents), and schedule a time for message delivery. The sender later receives an e-mail message reporting who answered the phone in person, whose message was received by an answering machine, and who was not reached. For those times users want a message to reach everyone in the database, it's possible to record a message and schedule a delivery time using just the telephone.

**Reliance Communications' SchoolMessenger Communications System:** www.schoolmessenger.com. SchoolMessenger Communications Systems are available for both site-based and centralized configurations. The site-based system is a USB plug-and-play arrangement featuring multilanguage messaging, automated calling, e-mail, and reporting. The centralized system is designed for a use with multiple school sites through a district. In addition to the site-based capabilities, the suite enables users to access other Web-based features. SchoolMessenger Communications Systems are installed in thousands of U.S. schools and send more than 250 million messages to parents each year.

**U.S. Netcom's PhoneMaster:** www.usnetcomcorp.com. U.S. Netcom Corporation targets several types of business and education communications needs, offering three products useful to schools or districts. PhoneMaster for Windows and PhoneMaster for Web enable users to communicate with parents and other staff members using the phone system, and PhoneMaster Priority Messaging is a low-cost alternative for sending just emergency messages. Visit the Web site to learn more about each system and to read some of the education success stories. Thousands of schools in the U.S. and around the world use U.S. Netcom systems.

## BEFORE MAKING A PURCHASE

There are several points that must be considered before choosing and implementing a technology-based communication system. The school's technology committee or another appropriate group must do some homework. First, the committee should gather specific data about the school community's access to telephones and the Internet. Next, since many automated calling systems have the capability of transmitting messages in multiple languages, the committee should identify the primary language spoken in each student's home to develop a list of languages required. It's also important to find out parents' preferences for telephone contact (home or work, day or evening) and whether they prefer e-mail or phone contact. Some parents are unable to receive personal calls at work except in extreme emergencies, while other parents prefer to have calls made or e-mails sent to their businesses during the day so that their children cannot intercept them. Gathering this information will help the committee determine the type of system and the features needed to best serve the school and parents.

At this point, the entire school staff should be brought into the discussion to decide how much effort they are willing to make in system implementation. Who will use the system and for what purpose? Does the committee envision a tool primarily for office staff use? Will teachers be asked to assume responsibilities related to system use, and, if so, what kind of time commitment will be required? It's easy to define limited use such as rumor control, school closure announcements, emergency announcements, or student absence verification, because most of this responsibility lies with the office. However, automated messaging systems have broader applications as well. For example, teachers can set up homework hotlines, maintain online grade reports, and share other classroom news with parents. Schools can also make regular announcements about extracurricular activities such as clubs or sports, special events, and fund raisers. Cantwell Sacred Heart of Mary High School, mentioned earlier in this chapter, has also had great success increasing parent participation in Back-to-School Night by using the school's automated system to send parents reminder messages about the event. In another instance, Principal David Chambers sent out a message regarding a food drive sponsored by the school, and within hours parents were bringing bags and boxes of food to the office. But in order to expand use in this way, staff members must agree to be regular users themselves in order to make the system pay off.

Once the committee has a clear picture of how the system will be used and the best means for communicating with the school community, members can research available systems to find the one that will support all the school's identified needs. In addition to speaking with vendors, check their Web sites for client lists or ask for a list of current users. Committee members can call several actual users to ask about strengths and weaknesses of the system and, if possible, visit a site where the system is installed to talk with staff and parents about how the system is used and whether they think it has been a wise investment.

The committee must also consider how to pay for the system. Some schools work with parent groups or local businesses to support the cost of the system. In these cases, the group or business may expect that each message will end with some sort of tag line stating, "This automated system is made possible by (name of the organization or business)." Would a statement of this type align with school policies regarding donations? The Diocese of Baton Rouge provides its schools an opportunity to reduce costs by opting into a diocesan contract which offers lower rates than schools could negotiate individually. Diocesan Superintendent Sr. Mary Michaeline, OP, explains that during the initial implementation year the diocese contributed $10,000 to fund the system and encouraged schools to work with their home/school associations as well. Smaller rural schools continue to receive financial support for the system through the diocese.

After the committee has selected a system, there's still more work to be done. Committee members must meet with staff and parents to develop and carry out an implementation plan. The plan must clearly define the purposes for the system and the parameters for appropriate use. Even though the chosen system may offer a number of communication options, it's helpful to add various uses incrementally. This allows you to learn the system thoroughly and find out which options work best for your community without overwhelming staff and parents. Overuse of the system by cluttering parents' e-mail or voice mail with inconsequential messages can be as off-putting as failing to provide promised services.

Finally, include strategies for keeping the telephone and e-mail database up to date and for protecting parents' privacy. In the spring of 2003, alumni and parents of students at Los Gatos High School in California received an e-mail message about an incident on campus from a community member who had no direct ties to the school. The message recipients were concerned because they believed this was an invasion of their privacy and a misuse of the school's directory of e-mail addresses. Although the community member refused to divulge how she accessed this information, administrators took immediate steps to make both the alumni list and the parent list more secure.

Using technology to spread important information quickly makes sense. While the school staff may not be able to outpace the grapevine, electronic communications systems can ensure that parents have access to accurate, timely information.

## ADDITIONAL RESOURCES

In addition to the resources cited above, you can learn more by accessing these online resources:

"School/Home Communication: Using Technology to Enhance Parental Involvement," at Center for the Study of Education Policy: http://www.illinois.net/pdf/ISU-STH-Study.pdf (January 2004). This study explores various ways to use technology-based communication with parents and discusses the challenges educators must anticipate.

Concept to Classroom, Making Family and Community Connections: http://www.thirteen.org/edonline/concept2class/familycommunity/index.html. Emergency notifications are important, but so are ongoing home/school communications. This online workshop is designed to help educators establish good working partnerships with parents and community members.

North Central Regional Educational Laboratory, Critical Issue: Creating the School Climate and Structures to Support Parent and Family Involvement: http://www.ncrel.org/sdrs/areas/issues/envrnmnt/famncomm/pa300.htm. Why focus on home/school communication? Review the resources in this NCREL Pathway to learn more about the impact of good communication and parental involvement in schools.

U.S. Department of Education Emergency Planning, Lead & Manage My School: http://www.ed.gov/admins/lead/safety/emergencyplan/index.html. Effective emergency communication requires advance planning. Use the resources on this site to anticipate ways your school can deal with home/school communication in emergencies.

## QUESTIONS FOR DISCUSSION

1. Describe strategies your school/district uses for regular and emergency home/school communication.

2. What role does technology use currently play in both kinds of home/school communication at your location? Explain.

3. In your opinion, how effective is your school/district system of home/school communication? Explain.

4. How could home/school communication be improved? Explain.

5. What is the role of administrators in home/school communication?

6. What is the role of teaching staff in home/school communication?

7. Would the messaging systems described in this chapter work for your school/district? Explain.

# 23

# *Assistive Technologies*

## *Meeting the Needs of Students With Physical Disabilities*

> Most educators are aware of equal access concerns related to issues such as gender, socioeconomic factors, and the like. Fewer realize that equal access requirements also impact children with various disabilities. In fact, due to laws that protect these children, this is more than an ethics concern. This chapter discusses some of the issues and potential solutions.

A high school student decides to conduct independent online research for a class project. Not an unusual scenario, but this student has low vision. Fortunately, she has access to a computer system that has an antiglare screen and a screen magnifier, making it possible for her to read the text displayed on the monitor. The computer also has a keyboard with large labels, facilitating data entry as she takes notes.

An elementary student is learning how to use a new software program. The program provides audio signals designed to let users know when

SOURCE: *Today's School*, May/June 2004

they've made a mistake, but this student has a profound hearing loss. It's not a problem for him, however, because the computer he uses has a special software program installed. Every time an audio signal is emitted, the computer screen flashes to alert him that audio feedback has been provided.

A middle school student needs to write a report for his social studies class. A diving accident has left him a quadriplegic, but there's nothing wrong with his voice. Using speech recognition software and a microphone, he is able to dictate and edit his report.

How well would these same students fare in a classroom at your site? Amendments made to the Individuals with Disabilities Education Act (IDEA) in 1997 prohibit setting a separate education agenda for students with special needs and hold educators accountable for ensuring that these students show progress in the general education program. Additional amendments in 2004 align the act with No Child Left Behind regulations that require that all but the most profoundly disabled students (approximately 1 percent) be tested to measure their academic progress using the same grade-level appropriate assessments taken by other students. For educators working with students who have physical disabilities, often the first step in meeting these guidelines is figuring out how to make the general academic program available to students who, due to hearing or vision loss or to orthopedic disabilities, need additional support just to get to the instructional starting gate. Working with children who face these challenges can tax the limits of general education teachers who often have little training in how to include these students. Advances in assistive technologies can help teachers transform these students' learning experiences from passive observation to active participation.

## WHAT ARE ASSISTIVE TECHNOLOGIES?

*Assistive technologies* are products including hardware and software programs that enable students with a variety of disabilities to function more independently in the classroom and to learn more effectively. Literally thousands of assistive technologies are available to make everyday activities accessible to these students. While the broad definition of assistive technologies includes devices designed to support students with learning disabilities as well as physical disabilities, this chapter focuses on assistive technologies designed for use by students with physical disabilities.

So what kinds of technologies are available? In addition to the examples already mentioned, there are

- Alternative keyboards with extra-sensitive keys, overlays, or other modifications, including virtual or onscreen keyboards, that facilitate data entry
- Data entry devices including head-mounted mice, electronic pointing devices, or trackballs

- Screen review software that works with a speech synthesizer, and document readers that use flatbed scanners and speech synthesizers, to make on- and off-line print materials accessible

This is just a small sampling. Several of the sites mentioned later in this chapter are excellent resources for learning about additional types of assistive technologies.

## WHERE CAN I LEARN MORE ABOUT PROVIDING ACCESS?

When writing an Individual Education Plan (IEP) for a student, the plan must include a description of any supplementary aids or accommodations that will be provided to enable the student to access the general education program. The Utah State Office of Education offers a link to an online area that can be very helpful to educators working with students with disabilities. The area, called Student Accommodations and Interventions: Aims for Success, can be accessed at www.usoe.k12.ut.us/sars/Links_Resources/InstStrat.htm, and includes tools such as matrices that can be used to identify the kinds of accommodations and supplementary aids that can be included in an IEP. This is especially helpful for educators who aren't sure where to start when identifying possible accommodation strategies and assistive technologies. The Alliance for Technology Access (www.ataccess.org/resources/atk12/default.html) also offers planning tools and showcases best practices. Other online resources that provide a wide array of materials helpful in planning for providing access to the general curriculum include the Access Center (www.k8accesscenter.org), and the Center for Applied Special Technology, or CAST (www.cast.org).

## WHERE CAN I LEARN MORE ABOUT SPECIFIC ASSISTIVE TECHNOLOGIES?

With thousands of assistive technologies now available, there are a number of vendors who sell a variety of products. You will need to gather information from several different companies to compare information about range of products, pricing, and customer support and service. Here are links to a few vendors to start with:

- **Assistive Technologies, Inc.:** www.assistivetechnologies.com. This company offers assistive technologies for users with vision, hearing, speech, mobility, and learning disabilities.
- **EnableMart, Technology for Everyone:** www.enablemart.com. In addition to a variety of assistive technologies, EnableMart sells

workstations and furniture designed to make technology more accessible to users with disabilities.

- **NanoPac, Inc.:** www.nanopac.com. NanoPac products and services primarily target persons with low vision, blindness, quadriplegia, and hearing impairments. Other kinds of assistive technologies are available as well.

For those who wish to do additional research on their own, the ABLEDATA Web site (www.abledata.com/) is very helpful. The National Institute on Disability and Rehabilitation Research, a part of the U.S. Department of Education's Office of Special Education and Rehabilitative Services, sponsors this site. Visitors can access a searchable database of more than 20,000 currently available assistive technology products, read consumer comments about products, access articles about assistive technology, and more. A similar resource is AbilityHub (www.abilityhub.com). The site uses categorized links to help visitors find information about specific types of assistive technologies. You are also invited to contact the site with brief questions, which will be answered via e-mail.

## ADDITIONAL POINTS TO CONSIDER

Making assistive technologies available is important, but you also must consider the school's physical environment. How are classrooms, library/media centers, and other learning centers arranged? Students with mobility or vision disabilities must be offered a physical environment that allows them to move easily and safely around classrooms and buildings. Workstations that are easily accessible and will accommodate wheelchairs, or are ergonomically sound for students with mobility disabilities, are also needed. All the assistive technology in the world won't help if the student can't get to it.

You also should make sure your school's Web site is accessible to persons with disabilities. While Section 508 of the Rehabilitation Act Amendments of 1998 is not currently applied to schools, if use of the school's Web site is an integral part of your curriculum, then all students must be afforded access. The Center for Applied Special Technology developed an online tool, called Bobby, for testing Web sites for accessibility. Now called *WebXACT*, and available through Watchfire at http://webxact.watchfire.com/, you can use this free service to identify potential accessibility issues on your site. A commercial version is available for purchase.

Finally, don't forget professional development. Teachers will require support in learning how to use the assistive technologies themselves before they will be comfortable having students use them. Training should also include strategies for using the assistive technologies to make accommodations in instruction for students with disabilities.

# ADDITIONAL RESOURCES

In addition to the resources cited above, you can learn more by accessing these online resources:

AT Network: http://www.atnet.org/. Resources and information for children and adults. Some topics are California-specific, but still a good resource for all.

Center for Assistive Technology & Environmental Access: http://www.catea.org/. News, publications, and resources about assistive technologies.

Council for Exceptional Children: http://www.ideapractices.org/. This international professional organization works to improve education for children with exceptionalities of all kinds. The site offers a variety of resources for educators.

U.S. Department of Education, Special Education & Rehabilitative Services: http://www.ed.gov/policy/speced/guid/idea/idea2004.html. Information about the Individuals with Disabilities Education Improvement Act of 2004.

University at Buffalo, School of Public Health and Health Professions, Assistive Technology Training Online Project: http://atto.buffalo.edu/. Information, resources, and tutorials focusing on use of assistive technologies at the elementary school level.

## QUESTIONS FOR DISCUSSION

1. Based upon your reading, define the term *assistive technology*.

2. Describe steps taken at your site/district to ensure that the general academic program is accessible to students with disabilities.

3. How is technology used to support these efforts?

4. List the assistive technologies currently available to your students.

5. What accommodations are teachers at your site/district making to ensure that students with physical disabilities are able to use technology?

6. Is your school/district Web site accessible to students with disabilities? Explain.

7. What kinds of professional development are available to teachers and staff at your site/district who work with students who have disabilities?

# 24

# Sitting Pretty?

## The Ergonomics of Computer Workstations

> By introducing various technologies into school offices and classrooms, we have also introduced the need to reconsider and redesign work spaces to ensure the ongoing physical health of adults and students. Because of their supervisory responsibilities, administrators must raise their own awareness of ergonomics issues related to technology use and make every effort to see that staff and children understand safe usage practices. This chapter will help you get started.

You know when you add computers to the office, lab, or classroom that you must put aside additional funds for equipment upgrades, software, staff development, technical support, and infrastructure needs, including electrical service. But what kind of work environment do you create when the new equipment is installed? Do adult staff members work at stations designed for comfort and efficiency or are new systems placed on desks purchased 20 years ago? Are students sitting on adjustable chairs at tables that are the correct height and offer keyboard and mouse trays, or are they making do in a one-size-fits-all setting?

SOURCE: *Today's School*, February 2002

Ergonomically sound work areas are becoming a concern for both adults and students, particularly as technology use in schools increases. The physical effects of long-term computer use in adults are well documented. Pain in the back, neck, and shoulders; hand and wrist problems; headaches; and eyestrain are all known results of poor posture, incorrectly designed office furniture, and failing to take frequent breaks from keyboard work.

Do children run the same risks as they increase their computer use? The answer to this question is not yet clearly defined, but experts are beginning to look more closely at the physical effects on students who are spending longer periods of time working at computers. What impact might this have on schools as they increase office automation and decrease their student-to-computer ratio? This chapter explores some of the issues and solutions surrounding ergonomics in the office and the classroom.

## IN THE OFFICE

Anyone using a computer for a prolonged period of time needs access to a properly placed keyboard and mouse, a comfortable chair that provides back support, a properly positioned monitor, and appropriate lighting. In most office environments these needs can be met by purchasing specially designed furniture and work lamps. A wise school administrator now includes costs for workstation furniture and lighting when calculating total cost of ownership and makes appropriate purchases when new equipment is ordered.

What does an ideal workstation provide? A comfortable, adjustable chair is a must. At the minimum, the user needs to be able to change the height of the chair and the back support position. Pivoting armrests with adjustable height and width settings are desirable. Keyboard trays that are height adjustable and at a negative slope allow users to maintain a posture that causes less stress to arms and wrists. Desktop keyboards and trays on a positive slope may actually contribute to wrist extension and injuries. A mouse tray or platform allows the user to position the mouse close to the side of the body and above the keyboard.

The monitor position is important as well. The screen needs to face the user directly and the top of the monitor should be two to three inches above the user's line of sight. The user's distance from the monitor needs to be approximately one arm's length, and bifocal wearers will be more comfortable if the monitor is tilted slightly backward. If the text on the screen is too small for users to read, they should increase the font size while working, not move the monitor closer.

Good lighting illuminates the work area without causing glare on the screen. If work lamps are used, they should be positioned so that the user cannot see the light source while looking at the monitor. Antiglare screens are available, but good ones can be expensive, so it may be better to rearrange the workstation itself. Do not attempt to correct the problem by simply moving the monitor.

But what do you do about existing workstations that do not meet these basic needs? You need to begin retrofitting. Most office furniture companies sell adjustable keyboard trays and mouse platforms as separate accessories to be attached to existing desks and worktables. Monitor swivels for better placement are also available, and of course, chairs and lamps may be purchased individually. Over a period of time you can bring all your office workstations up to standard.

If an employees ask for devices to improve their workstations, do not ignore or put off responding to the request. Dealing with workplace injuries and compensation for them is time-consuming and expensive. Take care of preventable problems by being proactive and improving the work environment before there is a formal complaint.

In addition to providing a proper workstation, you need to encourage employees working at computers for several hours at a time to take frequent breaks, at least every 30 to 60 minutes. It's easy to get caught up in an online task and forget that you need to give your eyes a break or to do a couple of simple exercises to refresh yourself. There is now ergonomics software available, often freeware or shareware, designed to monitor computer use time and remind you to rest periodically. For more information about this type of software, visit the Healthy Computing site at www.healthycomputing.com/buyersguides/ergonomics_software.htm.

## IN THE CLASSROOM AND COMPUTER LAB

Most ergonomics studies focus on adult users, but children are very different from adults. Their size, body proportions, growth rates, daily activities, and developing muscular and skeletal systems all make it unwise to attempt to apply findings about adults to children. Therefore, it really isn't known how susceptible children may be to repetitive-stress injuries. Current conventional wisdom states that because children typically do not spend three to four hours daily using computers at school, if they are sustaining this kind of injury, it is probably due to home computer use where they have access to computers for longer periods of time. The same is probably also true for classroom teachers. Schools can provide a great service to young students by helping them acquire good work habits at the computer now so that these habits will last as they become teenagers and young adults. School officials should do what they can to make the environment healthier for students and to educate parents about workstation design at home.

Two of the most common problems in schools involve monitor placement and lighting. Computer monitors at schools are typically much higher than they need to be, causing students to strain both their eyes and necks as they look up to work. Lighting appropriate for a classroom is not necessarily appropriate for computer use, and school districts are seldom in a position to install indirect lighting systems in each classroom and lab to prevent glare on screens. These issues can be improved by placing monitors so the height more closely approximates students' eye level and through use of antiglare screen overlays on each monitor. Although quality antiglare screens can be costly, they are less expensive than installing a new lighting system.

Posture problems among students are also common. It is possible to purchase special computer furniture for classrooms and labs, but the challenge in creating an ergonomically sound workspace in these locations is great for several reasons. Students come in all shapes and sizes, and it is virtually impossible to design settings that will be appropriate for every single student. Adjustable chairs are the single biggest help, but at $200–$300 each, they simply aren't practical for most schools, and the time spent adjusting chairs for each student takes away from instructional time. Posture problems can be alleviated somewhat by placing keyboards on a flat surface at elbow level, and by locating the mouse right next to the keyboard; on the right for right-handed students, and on the left for left-handed students. Smaller students whose feet dangle when they sit at a computer station can be encouraged to put their backpacks on the floor under their feet for additional support.

## WHAT ABOUT LAPTOP COMPUTERS?

Many schools have laptop programs for both students and staff. While the portability and increased access to technology are definite bonuses, laptops are not well designed ergonomically. When the screen is at the appropriate height and distance, the keyboard and pointing device are not, and the reverse is true as well. Some adjustments can be made if you or students use laptops more than one hour at a time. For example, you can purchase an external keyboard, mouse, or monitor for extended use. Also, resist the temptation to use the laptop on a high desk or while lounging in an easy chair.

## WHAT IS THE BOTTOM LINE?

Keep in mind that you are dealing with two types of computer users: those who are at a keyboard more than three to four hours per day and those who are not. Those users who spend many hours at a computer are most likely adults who are using technology as part of their job. Their workstations must be designed for both safety and comfort, and little if any compromise is appropriate.

In the case of students and teachers who spend far less time sitting at a computer station, comfort is the key. Think about where equipment will be placed and who will use it most frequently and for what purpose, and keep ergonomics basics in mind when purchasing furniture or upgrading your facilities. Most important, realize that this issue will not disappear and that you need to stay current on ergonomics and schools. Cornell University maintains a Web site on ergonomics at CUErgo, http://ergo.human.cornell.edu.

## ADDITIONAL RESOURCES

In addition to the resources cited above, you can learn more by accessing these online resources:

Computer Ergonomics for Elementary School: http://www.orosha .org/cergos/. This site was developed through a grant from the Department of Consumer and Business Services, Oregon OSHA. Areas include an explanation of ergonomics; a discussion of what makes a good workstation, and good work habits.

"Ergonomics in the Computer Classroom" in *Encyclopedia of Educational Technology:* http://coe.sdsu.edu/eet/articles/ergonomics/index .htm (2003). This brief article discusses viewing distance and angle, chair design and height, and room lighting and ventilation.

Ergonomics for Children and Educational Environments: http:// education.umn.edu/kls/ecee/casestudies.html. This site offers guidelines, links to research, and information for teachers.

Ergonomics4Schools: http://www.ergonomics4schools.com/. A Web site for secondary students and teachers to use to learn more about healthy computing.

"Ergonomics for Schools," available online at http://www.lni.wa .gov/WorkplaceRights/files/ErgoSummaryStudentsandStaff.pdf. This two-page brochure offers good information for school employees and students.

## QUESTIONS FOR DISCUSSION

1. Are adult workstations in your site/district designed with ergonomics in mind? Explain.
2. Are student workstations in your site/district designed with ergonomics in mind? Explain.
3. What is the greatest impediment you face in providing ergonomically sound workstations for students and adults?
4. What can you do immediately to address this impediment?
5. A staff member complains about physical discomfort and mental fatigue related to extended periods of computer use. What steps would you take to address this complaint?
6. Describe steps you can take to educate parents about ergonomics concerns for children when using technology at home and at school.
7. Increasing numbers of schools are purchasing laptops rather than desktop computers. What ergonomics issues must be considered as students and teachers increase their use of laptops?

# *Index*

## CORWIN PRESS

The Corwin Press logo—a raven striding across an open book—represents the union of courage and learning. Corwin Press is committed to improving education for all learners by publishing books and other professional development resources for those serving the field of PreK–12 education. By providing practical, hands-on materials, Corwin Press continues to carry out the promise of its motto: **"Helping Educators Do Their Work Better."**